THE
DATING
RESET

A LATER DATER'S GUIDE TO ALIGNED LOVE

NADIA EDWARDS

© 2025 Nadia C. Edwards

All Rights Reserved

Published and printed in the United States of America.

This book is the property of Nadia C. Edwards. No part of this book may be reproduced, stored within a retrieval system, or transmitted in any form or by any means without the author's written permission except for the use of quotations in a book review, cited appropriately.

This is a work of nonfiction. Some names and identifying details have been changed to protect the privacy of individuals. Any resemblance to actual persons, living or dead, is purely coincidental.

Design by Ryan Mulford

Editing by Sage Taylor Kingsley

Paperback ISBN: **979-8-218-70399-8**

First Edition

Published by Walk Good Publishing

Walk Good Publishing is an imprint of Nadia C Edwards LLC

www.NadiaEdwards.com

Contents

Dedication	VI
INTRODUCTION: MY WAKE-UP CALL FOR ALIGNED LOVE	1
PHASE 1: DETACHMENT	8
CHAPTER 1: THE MOMENT OF TRUTH	9
CHAPTER 2: BREAKING THE FAIRY-TALE SPELL	22
CHAPTER 3: FACING YOUR EMOTIONAL PILE	33
PHASE 2: ALIGNMENT	44
CHAPTER 4: RECONNECTING WITH YOURSELF	45
CHAPTER 5: THE POWER OF LIVING ALIGNED LOVE	54
PHASE 3: TIME	70

CHAPTER 6:   71
THE DATING SABBATICAL

CHAPTER 7:   82
PATIENCE AND PERSPECTIVE

CHAPTER 8:   93
MAKING ROOM FOR LOVE

PHASE 4:   101
INTENTION

CHAPTER 9:   102
MOVING FROM FEAR TO INTENTION

CHAPTER 10:   111
VALUES-BASED DATING

CHAPTER 11:   122
THE EMPOWERED APPROACH

PHASE 5:   131
NURTURING

CHAPTER 12:   132
FILLING YOUR JOY CUP FIRST

CHAPTER 13:   142
RESILIENCE IN REJECTION

PHASE 6:   150
GRATITUDE

CHAPTER 14:   151
GRATITUDE AS A FOUNDATION

CHAPTER 15:   158
HONORING YOUR TRANSFORMATION

CONCLUSION: YOUR PATH TO LOVE	164
THANK YOUS	168
WORK WITH NADIA	170
ABOUT THE AUTHOR	173

To every woman who's had her heart broken,

this is for you, sis.

INTRODUCTION:
MY WAKE-UP CALL FOR ALIGNED LOVE

There's a moment in every woman's life when she stops, looks at her love life—or lack thereof—and asks herself, *How the fuck did I end up here?*

For me, that moment came when I hit my 40s. Heartbreak seemed more frequent than lasting love, and, yet again, I found myself grappling with the end of a relationship that I thought would last.

We had been together for about a year. He was an undercover cop—brave, mysterious, and with a certain edge that felt so familiar, it almost seemed comforting. I thought we had it all. We'd met each other's families and friends, talked about marriage, and merged our lives in ways that felt seamless. It was fast and intense, like something out of a romance movie.

And then, just before the holidays, he called me. The conversation started out routine, small talk about our days. But then he said six words that shattered my world: "I want to see other people."

The ground beneath me dissolved like quicksand. My heart pounded in my ears so loudly I thought I was having a heart attack. You see, his words didn't just mark the end of the relationship—I had to confront the reality that I had been chasing a fantasy. **I had mistaken his emotional distance for strength.**

And with those six words, like a house of dominoes, the illusion of safety—layered with fantasies, old patterns, and misplaced hopes came crashing down. In that moment, I realized something I had been avoiding for years: *I* was the common denominator in every failed relationship.

It wasn't just the men I had chosen: It was the patterns I had been holding onto. The fairy-tale ideals I repeatedly thought would save me. The unconscious pull toward emotionally unavailable men. And the cultural and family narratives that shaped my beliefs about love.

But here's the thing: realizing the truth doesn't change it overnight. There's no "Abracadabra!" Awareness is only the beginning. What followed was a journey—a process of letting go, rediscovery, and intentional transformation.

And this journey wasn't about finding the perfect man. It was about summoning the courage to release the past and create a new love story within me, aligned with my true self.

That breakup was my wake-up call.

It led me down an unexpected path: a yearlong dating sabbatical, deep reflection, and a transformation that didn't just change how I approached love—it reshaped how I understood it. I began to see love not as something to chase, but as something to create on my terms, guided by a vision of what love could truly be when it aligned with my values and my authentic self.

In the end, I didn't just redefine my approach to love—I lived it. I didn't just "get back out there"—I practiced dating with intention. At first, it felt unfamiliar, like a muscle I hadn't used in years. But with every date, I got clearer, more grounded, and more aligned with the kind of partnership I was calling in. I met a mix of men—some good, some not-so-good. But one stood out for all the right reasons. I chose him with my head first, because my heart had led me in the wrong direction before. Then, when I allowed my heart to enter, that's where I felt it - being seen, feeling safe, and completely at ease. He showed me consistency, care, and emotional availability. I wasn't waiting to be chosen this time. I chose the man who aligned with the love and life I had envisioned.

That man is now my husband. It feels easy to be together. We laugh a lot. We support each other's dreams. And when life gets hard, as it sometimes does, we show up as a team. No drama, no games, just a steady love rooted in shared values and mutual respect. It's the kind of relationship I didn't think was possible for me, but I'm so glad I stayed open to finding it.

This Book Is for You

When I decided to write this book, I thought back to the woman I was in my 40s, searching for love but fearful of another heartbreak, uncertain of where to look, and so weary of repeating the same choices. She wanted something different, something harmonious, but wasn't sure how to begin.

I wrote this for her. And I wrote it for you, if you've ever felt the same way. This book is your guide to redefining love on your terms, breaking free from what no longer serves you, and creating the kind of connection that feels authentic and aligned with who you truly are.

This book is not about quick fixes or finding "The One." It's about liberating yourself from old patterns that have been keeping you stuck, so you can redefine what love looks like for you, in this season of life. It's about dating with intention, understanding your values, and making new choices that are compatible with the life partnership you desire and deserve.

What You'll Learn

Throughout my story, I'll walk you through The Dating Reset Method—a clear, compassionate approach designed to help you release patterns, reconnect with yourself, and choose love with intention.

At the heart of this method is my signature D.A.T.I.N.G. framework:

(D) Detachment

Releasing patterns, limiting beliefs, and attachment styles that have been keeping you stuck. Detachment helps you free yourself from the fear of repeating past mistakes and create space for self-trust, emotional ease and new possibilities in love.

(A) Alignment

Choosing relationships that reflect your core values. Alignment ensures that your dating experience moves you toward, not away from, the kind of partnership you truly desire. It reduces the risk of misalignment and keeps you centered in what matters most.

(T) Time

Prioritizing your dating efforts and treating your love life with the same intentionality as other important goals. This approach helps you avoid the fear of wasting time or putting your desires on hold, and it also encourages you to focus on meaningful progress.

(I) Intention

Dating with curiosity and purpose, approaching each interaction mindfully. Intention reduces the fear of rejection and makes sure that your energy is spent cultivating connections that are emotionally rich and aligned.

(N) Nurturing

Prioritizing your overall well-being—emotional, mental, physical, and spiritual—as you date. Nurturing yourself through self-care and boundaries empowers you to stay grounded, engaged, and connected to yourself throughout the process.

(G) Gratitude

Reflecting on each step of your journey with an abundance mindset. Gratitude helps you find value and growth in every experience, releasing fear-based scarcity and embracing the lessons that lead to aligned love.

This is what the reset looks like. Each phase builds on the one before it, guiding you step by step—from emotional unlearning to emotional alignment, from passivity to purpose, from self-protection to genuine connection.

You'll start by letting go of what's been holding you back in **Phase 1: Detachment**, then root into what truly matters in **Phase 2: Alignment**.

Once your values are clear, **Phase 3: Time,** shows you how to prioritize the process of seeking a partner—giving it the same energy you give to other meaningful areas of your life, rather than treating it as something to squeeze in when everything else is handled.

From there, **Phase 4: Intention** helps you show up in dating with curiosity and clarity. To stay grounded, you'll move into **Phase 5: Nurturing**, where you'll learn to care for your whole self along the way.

Finally, in **Phase 6: Gratitude**, you'll reflect on the process with compassion and abundance.

Each chapter includes tools, mindset shifts, and reflective prompts designed to help you redefine love on your terms. Whether you're just starting to date again or have been on this path for years, these insights will meet you where you are and help you move forward with intention.

Here's the beautiful truth, sis: You can have love again, and it can be better than you ever dreamed of.

Ready? Let's get started.

PHASE 1:
DETACHMENT

"You take the red pill—you stay in Wonderland, and I show you how deep the rabbit hole goes."

— *Morpheus, The Matrix*

CHAPTER 1:
THE MOMENT OF TRUTH

There's nothing quite like heartbreak to bring your life into sharp focus.

When my relationship with the cop ended, I found myself on the floor of my bedroom, sobbing until my entire body ached. My chest felt like it was caving in, and the tears wouldn't stop. I could barely breathe, and the muffled hum of the ceiling fan above me felt cruelly indifferent to my pain.

Eventually, I dragged myself into bed, curling into the smallest version of myself I could manage. My sheets and comforter became my cocoon, the only place that felt safe. But even in my safe space, I couldn't escape the questions swirling in my mind: *How did this happen? Why does it keep happening? What's wrong with me?*

At first, I blamed him. He didn't value what we had. He never prioritized me. He wasn't ready for the love I was offering. I told myself that was the problem: him. But somewhere between gasping sobs and wiping snot-filled tears with the back of my hand, another thought crept in, one I'd been avoiding for years: *I was the common denominator in all my failed relationships.*

Connecting the Dots

That realization was almost too much to bear. Because it wasn't just about this one relationship—it was about every relationship I'd ever been in. For the first time, I started to see my patterns:

1. I was drawn to men who were confident, mysterious, and emotionally unavailable.

2. I confused emotional distance with strength, believing this reflected maturity or stability.

3. I didn't know what I really wanted or even what I should be looking for in a partner.

But here's the thing about patterns: They don't come out of nowhere. They're shaped by the stories we inherit, the beliefs we carry, and the experiences we live through.

Heartbreak in midlife carries a distinct kind of complexity, a blend of confidence and uncertainty that's both sobering and disorienting. On one hand, I had the confidence that came with age: years of life experiences, a clearer sense of who I was, and the hope that I'd learned enough to recognize what a healthy relationship looked like. But alongside that confidence was something harder to admit—a lingering uncertainty, a quiet question that refused to go away: *I'm a beautiful, smart, successful woman. Why does this keep happening?*

By midlife, we're all carrying the weight of our past relationships, the scars and lessons etched into who we are. And yet, when heartbreak strikes, those emotional piles can feel impossible to sort through.

How do we reconcile what we've been through with the hope of building something better?

It wasn't just the relationship I mourned—it was the hope I had pinned on it. At this stage in life, I still clung to the belief that love should come easily, like breathing. But midlife heartbreak forced me to confront the truth: Romantic love is rarely effortless. It takes time and the willingness to navigate the complexities of two lives flowing together, charting their course through both calm waters and turbulent currents.

Growing up, I had absorbed the belief that love was something you endured, not something that sustained you. Independence became a badge of honor, a way of navigating a world where vulnerability felt too risky.

In that moment, I realized I wasn't just choosing emotionally unavailable men: *I was replicating the emotional distance I had been raised with.*

As I understood it, love wasn't about connection or mutual support. It was about survival.

The Wake-Up

That breakup didn't just leave me shattered - it cracked something open. I'd already cried all the tears. I'd already asked all the questions. But now, wrapped in my cocoon of blankets, something shifted. The wake-up happened. I didn't know the way forward yet, but I suddenly knew that if I wanted a different kind of love, I had to start making different choices.

No instant fix. Just a decision to stop running on autopilot and start unpacking the beliefs and behaviors that kept me stuck, like watching reruns of the same plot play out in my life—just with different-looking men.

My vision for love, the choices I was making, and the patterns I kept repeating were out of sync with who I was and what I truly desired.

That realization hit me like a tidal wave. And with that flood of awareness came fear, denial, and, ultimately, acceptance. Because here's the truth: Awareness doesn't fix the problem—it simply shines a light on it.

That moment wasn't about finding the answers. It was about recognizing the disconnection and starting to reconnect the dots in a way that aligned with the real me - not the version shaped by past experiences, societal expectations, or the pressures of family ideals.

The Journey Begins

That moment of truth marked the beginning of what I now call my *journey of redefining love.*

In that moment, I didn't have a detailed plan or a step-by-step guide. I didn't know how to break the patterns I had carried for so long or how to let go of the fairy-tale ideals and cultural narratives that had shaped my expectations. I didn't fully understand what lay ahead.

But I knew one thing for sure: I had to try.

And I knew that something had to change, and that change had to start with me.

I made the bold decision to take a year-long dating sabbatical, work with a dating coach, and dive deep into self-reflection to understand the patterns that had been preventing me from having the love life I truly desired.

It wasn't easy, and it wasn't fast. There were moments of doubt and discomfort—moments when I thought: *WTF am I doing? Can I really change? Am I capable of finding a man who can truly meet me where I am? Someone different, someone better?*

But despite the questions and uncertainty, I kept going. And it was worth it.

Once I re-entered dating, I did it differently, this time with intention. Not with fingers crossed, hoping maybe this will work out, but with clarity, curiosity, and a strategy that actually reflected what I wanted.

Now, full transparency, it wasn't a smooth start. My coach told me: "First dates should be short. No meals. Just meet him in person for proof of life and to see if there's any physical attraction. If there's mutual interest, then decide if there should be a second date." So … what did I do? I had a whole meal. Eating is basically my love language, and I wasn't about to sip a quick latte. I wanted vibes and fries.

But even with a few stumbles, I showed up differently. I used a mix of dating apps and in-person events, stayed open, and asked questions that reflected my values. I didn't just want a relationship—I wanted alignment.

Once I settled into what I'd learned from my dating coach, something clicked. I gave myself a focused window to apply it all—dating with self-awareness, curiosity, and intention.

And that's when I met him.

I knew that part of dating successfully also meant just getting out of the house. Going to the kinds of places where my life partner might also go, places where I would enjoy going regardless if I met someone or not. So on my first month back in the dating pool, I went on about 20+ dates—some with men, some solo. But even the solo dates weren't about "waiting" or "preparing"—they were part of the process. I made space on my calendar for dating, period. Whether it was dinner with someone new or taking myself to the art museum (my favorite solo date spot), I stayed open.

I moved with intention, and once I sensed a genuine connection, I made it clear: I was looking for a life partner and actively dating to find someone aligned. That level of honesty helped me see who was actually ready for something real. I chatted, met, observed, and decided.

And if it wasn't a good fit, I didn't take it personally. I didn't analyze what he did or didn't do. I thanked him for his time, appreciated the opportunity to connect, and moved on. See, we're all just looking for our person, and realizing that softened how I approached meeting men. It wasn't about judgment—it was about clarity.

Out of all the dates during that time, he stood out. Not because of instant fireworks, but because I was paying attention in a different way. He was consistent. He made me laugh. He had passion, vision, and emotional availability. And most importantly, he reflected the values I had identified as non-negotiable: trust, integrity, humor, and consistency. He wasn't trying to rush into something, and neither was I—we were both genuinely curious about each other.

In 2025, we'll celebrate five years of a marriage that still feels both exhilarating and sacred.

It wasn't luck. It wasn't magic.

It was mindset. It was discernment.

It was choosing to believe that aligned love was possible and being ready to recognize it when it arrived. Alignment doesn't mean perfect. It means solid. It means steady. It means choosing someone who's already dialed into the life and love you've envisioned, not someone you hope can fit into it.

So if you're thinking, "That could never happen for me," I get it. I used to think that, too. And now, I hear it from my clients all the time. But I also know that many of us secretly crave the kind of relationship we see happen for others; we just haven't been taught how to believe it's truly available to us. **The truth is: it is.**

It starts with belief. That belief is strengthened by practice. And when the man who actually complements your life and shares your values shows up, *he might not look like what you imagined, but he'll be exactly what you need.*

The process of redefining love was deeply rewarding—a journey that brought me closer to the kind of love, and the kind of life, I truly desired.

The Loop:

"This is just the type of man I'm drawn to."

For a long time, I didn't realize I was gravitating toward men who couldn't meet me emotionally, weren't clear about what they wanted, or kept me at arm's length. It wasn't a conscious choice. That pull felt natural, but it was really just familiar. I was repeating a pattern without realizing it, chasing connection where there was no real capacity for it.

The Reset:

"Attraction isn't fixed. I can choose differently by watching what's real."

Instead of following a familiar feeling, I started paying attention to behavior. Was he consistent? Did his words match his actions? Was he emotionally available in the ways I needed? The more I observed, the more I recalibrated what I found attractive. That's when everything changed.

The belief I shared is just one of many I had to reframe. Most of my clients go through this, too.

Take Vanessa, who realized how often she mistook chemistry for a romantic connection. For years, she believed:

"Instant attraction is enough. When I feel it, that means he's the right one for me."

But that belief kept her stuck in the same loop—dating men who brought excitement but also left her feeling anxious and unsure. Through our work together, she came to a new understanding:

"I need to trust myself more, knowing that I'm in a more informed position than I was before. The one thing I learned from my past is attraction is not enough: Alignment is the key. Moving forward, I've got to ask more questions tied to my values."

She realized that the kind of attraction she had relied on in the past felt like fireworks—**exhilarating at first, but always followed by a crash.** What she truly needed was something more grounded, more lasting, more real.

In the chapters that follow, I'll take you through the process I went through, unpacking emotional piles, rediscovering my values, and learning to date with intention.

The journey to aligned love starts with awareness, and awareness starts with a moment of truth.

Key Takeaways:

- Heartbreak is not just an ending, it's also an opportunity to reflect and reset.

- Awareness of patterns is the first step toward redefining your approach to love.

- A wake-up call doesn't solve everything, but it marks the start of your transformative journey.

Reflection Exercise:

- Write down 3-5 patterns you've noticed in your past relationships. These could be patterns about the type of partner you chose, the level of relationship commitment and connection, and/or how you felt and acted while in that relationship.

- Reflect on how these patterns have shaped your approach to love. Consider the role your beliefs may have played in creating or sustaining these patterns.

- Identify one belief about love that you want to let go of, and journal about why. What is a new belief you'd like to embody instead of that?In the next chapter, we'll explore why I was so drawn to a fictional character—James Bond—and the impact of fairy tales on how we learn to love.

CHAPTER 1:

CHAPTER 2:
BREAKING THE FAIRY-TALE SPELL

"Shaken, not stirred."

James Bond had me hooked from the first moment I saw him on screen, as a young girl. Sure, the tailored suits, piercing eyes, and effortless charm didn't hurt. But it wasn't just the physical allure that drew me in—it was what he represented. Bond was everything I thought a man should be. Strong. Confident. Always in control.

Watching Bond navigate life-and-death situations without so much as breaking a sweat made me feel safe, like no problem was too big for him to handle. He wasn't just a suave spy; he was the embodiment of reliability and composure, qualities I wanted in a partner.

At the time, I didn't realize how much my fascination with Bond and the romantic ideals I'd absorbed from movies and TV were shaping how I approached love. But Bond didn't appear out of nowhere. He wasn't just a fantasy; on some level, he felt like an antidote to the relationship stories I'd grown up hearing and observing.

The Values We Inherit

In my family, conversations about men were rarely flattering. Growing up, the stories I overheard, or was told, painted men as anything but dependable. Many were more like gigolos, offering empty promises and leaving behind generations of fatherless daughters. I was one of them.

My father wasn't entirely absent; he popped in once in a while, just enough to keep hope alive. And what I remember most was this inconsistency. The promises he made and didn't keep. The times he said he'd be back and wasn't.

Such broken promises hit differently at a young age. They create a wound that doesn't bleed or swell but still hurts deeply. It lingers quietly, conforming how we expect to be loved by men.

And from my lens, those stories I heard around me about men who didn't show up, who disappointed, who left—only solidified my own experience. They didn't feel like cautionary tales. They felt like confirmation. They reinforced what I had lived, and made the stories of the women in my family feel undeniably true.

These weren't just idle conversations; they carried the hard-earned wisdom of generations; beliefs shaped by disappointment, survival, and resilience. Whether intentional or not, those beliefs were passed down to me; but they didn't come through stories alone. I was living inside them.

My once-every-few-years father, the broken promises, the silence—I wasn't just hearing about men who couldn't be counted on, I was experiencing it firsthand.

And while I didn't know it at the time, I had absorbed deeply rooted beliefs about love, relationships, and what I could expect from men. All this became part of the values stew I grew up consuming, quietly shaping how I saw men and what I believed was possible.

Whether it was whispered conversations over Sunday dinners or the matter-of-fact tone when they spoke of men who left, cheated, or simply didn't show up, the message was clear: Men could not be relied on.

Here are a few of those unconscious beliefs and what I now know to be true:

Old Beliefs I Carried:

- Love means waiting for him to choose me.

- Men leave, so I'd better not get too attached.

- A strong woman doesn't need a man, so I shouldn't expect much.

- When it's the right man, I'll feel a spark or instant chemistry.

- I have to earn and keep a man's love by being easygoing and undemanding.

What I Now Believe:

- Love is a mutual, intentional choice.

- A real connection unfolds over time and deepens through alignment.

- Being soft and open doesn't make me weak, it makes me ready.

- Sometimes the spark is a signal that I'm repeating something.

- I don't have to perform to be loved. I just have to be me.

The Problem with Fantasies

The problem with action/romance movies and fantasies is that they set us up for failure. They teach us to prioritize that electric first-glance feeling over compatibility, to mistake sex for love, and to ignore the warning signs when something isn't right.

For years, I chased that fantasy without realizing it. I was drawn to men who seemed to embody the qualities I admired in Bond—charisma, independence, and toughness because that resonated with the emotionally and physically avoidant patterns I had seen in childhood. Men with those qualities made me feel safe in the moment, but intimacy never went beyond the surface.

I wasn't choosing. I was following a script, unaware that I was in a story that had been handed down to me.

Recognizing the Subconscious Pull

It took years and a lot of heartbreak for me to understand why I was drawn to those men. Looking back, it's no surprise. The relationships I was chasing mirrored the dynamics I grew up with.

And it wasn't just my parents' relationship that shaped me. Across my extended family, uncles left, cousins were raised without fathers, women rarely spoke of their hurt but suffered from it anyway—there was a pattern. A quiet, generational knowing that love from men was inconsistent at best, and painful at worst.

I saw the women in my family carry it all. My mother and my aunts moved through life with a kind of unspoken resilience. They paid the bills, raised the children, worked long hours, and kept it all together. I don't recall ever seeing my mother or other grown women cry when I was growing up. The message was clear: hold it in, handle it yourself, and keep moving.

The men? Some were physically present, but not emotionally supportive. Others disappeared altogether. Dependability wasn't expected, it was optional. Love wasn't a soft place; it was something to be suspicious of. And any talk of needing a man, or worse, depending on one, was met with side eye or a half-joke that said: "Girl, you should know better."

Vulnerability wasn't just discouraged; it was viewed as a weakness. My mother, like many women in our Caribbean culture, wore her independence like armor. She handled everything on her own, and I learned to do the same.

As a girl, I couldn't name what I was learning, but I felt it in my core. I saw romantic love as something you had to earn by keeping the house clean, by staying strong, and by never asking for too much. And as a woman, I craved affection from men but didn't know how to ask for it. So I learned to perform in the way I was conditioned, hoping it would lead to being chosen.

Breaking Free from the Spell

The moment I realized how much these fantasies and the values and beliefs behind them had shaped my choices, I knew I had to let them go. But letting go of a fantasy isn't easy; it's like trying to swim through murky water, the false promises clinging to you like heavy chains.

The fantasy whispers: "Stay a little longer. It's safer here." It wraps around you, offering comfort even as it keeps you stuck. But with every stroke forward, the illusion fades, and you move closer to clarity, to freedom, to the love and life that aligns with your truth.

For me, the shift started with redefining what love meant. I began to ask myself:

- Does my ideal of love serve me, or does it limit me?

- Am I chasing chemistry at the expense of compatibility?

- How can I create a vision of love that aligns with MY true core values, not just the ones I inherited?

Building a New Vision

As I worked through these questions, I stopped looking for men who had 007 energy and started looking for partners who valued connection, vulnerability, and mutual respect—more Sterling K. Brown, Morris Chestnut, or Taye Diggs than James Bond.

It wasn't about abandoning standards; it was about raising them in a way that reflected my true desires.

Instead of focusing on how a man looked or whether he checked all the boxes, I focused on *how he made me feel* and whether he consistently aligned with my core values, **in his actions, not just his words**—because sometimes, the love we truly desire doesn't come in the package we expect. He might not match the fairy tale we imagined or even the type we've always been drawn to (age, race, height, physique, personality), but that doesn't make the connection any less real or meaningful.

One of the most surprising lessons I learned was that love doesn't always feel like fireworks. Sometimes, it feels like a steady flame—something solid, consistent, and grounded. And in the end, that's exactly what I needed.

My new definition of love?

It's mutual. It's grounded. It's safe in the ways that matter.

It looks like shared values, follow-through, and honest conversations, even when they're uncomfortable.

It feels like ease, not confusion.

Love now feels less like proving myself and more like being myself... and being accepted fully.

Key Takeaways:

- Romantic fantasies, while comforting, can create unrealistic expectations that prevent you from finding true connection.

- The stories and values you inherit about love play a significant role in shaping your relationship patterns.

- Letting go of familial and societal concepts about love allows you to embrace a healthier, more aligned and sustainable vision of love.

Reflection Exercise:

- List 2-3 ideals you've held about love or relationships. They may have originated in your family of origin, friend group, religious community, or media. Think of the messages you absorbed about what love is supposed to feel like or look like. These beliefs can be subtle—like: "If it's meant to be, it should be effortless," or "If he really loves me, he'll just know what I need." Earlier, I shared mine:

the fantasy of a James Bond-type man—smooth, independent, tough, and emotionally hard to read. Take a moment to reflect on your own. Write them down.

- Reflect on how these have influenced your choices in partners. What patterns have you noticed in who you're attracted to, what you overlook, or what you prioritize? Are there recurring dynamics that feel familiar—even if they haven't served you? Remember, this is about self-awareness, not self-blame. You're connecting the dots so you can rewrite the story.

- Write a new definition of love that aligns with your values and emotional needs. Think about what love feels like when it's healthy, what it looks like when it's real, and what behaviors build that kind of connection. I shared my definition earlier in this section, but please take a moment to think about your own. What would a relationship rooted in mutual care, shared values, and emotional clarity look like for you? What would it feel like? This isn't about getting the words perfect—it's about getting honest with yourself.

In the next chapter, we'll look at what I call the emotional pile: all the unprocessed feelings, stories, and memories that might be influencing your dating life more than you realize.

CHAPTER 3:
FACING YOUR EMOTIONAL PILE

The Stories We Carry

In the household I grew up in, grounded in Jamaican culture, "Ah suh dem stay" was a phrase I heard more times than I can count anytime men were being discussed. Loosely translated, it means, "That's just how they are." It was a way to brush off, acknowledge, and quietly condone men's shortcomings without dwelling on the hurt. As a child, I accepted it as truth, not yet questioning what it meant for my own understanding of love.

Hearing this phrase sent a clear message: Expecting more from a man was setting yourself up for disappointment. It molded my early understanding of love as something you tolerated, not something that sustained or uplifted you. But looking back now, I wonder if the women around me even knew what "more" could look like or if they'd ever seen it for themselves. Or even believed it was possible.

Their stories and lives rarely included examples of healthy, supportive relationships. Instead, they spoke of compromise and survival. The idea of expecting emotional support, mutual respect, or shared responsibility wasn't part of their vocabulary—not because they didn't deserve it, but because it wasn't something they had seen or experienced.

These narratives didn't just inform me; they were tossed onto me, starting an emotional pile. Beliefs, expectations, and unspoken rules about love accumulated there, influencing how I understood relationships and the choices I made in partners.

On one hand, my family's stories spoke of love as a survival tool—something tied to duty, responsibility, and endurance. On the other hand, the passionate storybook love I saw in movies offered an intoxicating contrast.

The movies promised grand gestures and happily-ever-afters, filled with bliss, partnership, and joy. But these stories clashed with what I saw and heard at home, where love was rarely about happiness. Instead, it was about resilience, sacrifice, and making do.

I felt torn between those two worlds. Part of me wanted to believe in the magic of romantic love—love that felt like fireworks and forever. Yet, another part whispered that this kind of love wasn't meant for women like me, shaped by the narratives passed down through generations.

This tension left me clinging to the fantasy. We all want to be happy, don't we? And for me, the storybook ideal felt like a glimmer of hope—a promise that love could be something more than survival. Even if it seemed out of reach, it was worth chasing.

But the stories we inherit from our families shape us in ways we don't always recognize. For me, the contrasting narratives of love—the practical lessons from my family and the romantic ideals from the screen—created a tug-of-war in my heart. Over time, these conflicting influences became part of my emotional pile—an accumulation of beliefs, experiences, and narratives that subtly, yet powerfully, guided how I approached love.

Emotional Distance as a Survival Tool

Earlier, I shared how independence was modeled as a form of survival. But it wasn't until I began unpacking my emotional pile that I saw just how deeply that survival mode lived in me.

Looking back, I wasn't just acting strong. I was avoiding vulnerability. I equated asking for help with weakness. And without realizing it, I began building my relationships around that same emotional distance. Emotional expression wasn't something we talked about; it was something we suppressed. There was too much to be done to make room for vulnerability.

This wasn't just a survival tool; it was a barrier. It kept me from forming deep, meaningful connections. And it made me unconsciously seek out partners who were just as emotionally unavailable as I was.

Unpacking Attachment Styles

> *"Understanding attachment styles is the single most important thing you can do to improve your relationships. Once you learn about them, your relationships will never be the same again."*
> —Dr. Amir Levine & Rachel Heller

One of the most powerful ways to help sort through your emotional piles is to explore your attachment style.

These styles rooted in our earliest caregiving experiences act like blueprints for how we relate to others as adults. As Dr. Amir Levine and Rachel Heller explain in *Attached*, early relationships with caregivers create a roadmap for how we approach intimacy and connection.

The good news? These patterns aren't fixed. With awareness and intentional shifts, we can move toward more secure, fulfilling relationships.

Here's a quick overview of the four primary attachment styles:

1. **Secure**: You feel comfortable with intimacy and independence, trusting your partner without fear of abandonment or losing yourself.

2. **Anxious**: You crave closeness and often fear rejection or

abandonment, leading to a need for constant reassurance.

3. **Avoidant**: You value independence and often feel uncomfortable with emotional closeness, leading to a tendency to pull or push away.

4. **Fearful-Avoidant (Disorganized)**: You experience a mix of anxious and avoidant tendencies, desiring connection but fearing it at the same time. Come closer, go away.

Understanding your attachment style isn't about blame, it's about awareness.

Breaking the Cycle

It took me years to recognize these inherited cycles and how they were keeping me stuck in the loop. The self-sufficiency I had admired in the women in my life had become a double-edged sword. It helped me survive, but it also taught me to protect instead of connect.

But here's the thing: Your emotional pile doesn't have to define you. Once I became aware of my avoidant style patterns, I realized I had the power to change them.

For me, breaking the cycle started with reflection. I had to take a hard look at the stories I'd inherited: the ones that told me men couldn't be relied on, that vulnerability was a weakness, and that love was something to endure rather than enjoy.

I had to ask myself three questions:

1. Do these stories, or some portion of them, still serve me?

2. Which ones do I need to let go of?

3. How can I create a new narrative that aligns with who I am today?

Our attachment styles are not locked in stone. As we gain self-awareness and make new choices of partners, and we communicate and fill our own emotional needs better, we can evolve to loving in a more secure way and being more attracted to secure partners.

Steps Toward Healing

Sorting through your emotional pile is a lot like cleaning out your closet. It's not about erasing the past, but about carefully deciding what to keep and what to let go of. Some pieces might still fit but no longer reflect your style, while others—no matter how long you've held onto them—just aren't your size anymore. Letting go of those outdated pieces isn't always easy, but it's the only way to make room for what truly suits and supports the person you are now.

Practical Steps for Sorting through Your Emotional Pile

Here are some steps you can take to begin sorting through your own emotional pile:

1. **Identify patterns in your relationships**: What kinds of partners are you drawn to? How do they reflect the emotional dynamics you grew up with? They may be the same as what was modeled for you, or the opposite.

2. **Allow yourself to be vulnerable:** Yes, it's a risk. But it's also a power move. Real connection can't happen without it, and the love you want won't grow within a concrete-encased heart. That said, vulnerability doesn't have to mean spilling everything at once—try it in small doses, with discernment. Pay attention to how it's received. Trust is built, not assumed.

3. **Seek support**: Whether it's a coach or therapist, having someone walk alongside you as you unpack your beliefs about romantic love and partnership can help you see your blind spots, challenge old narratives, and create new possibilities.

Let's go back to Vanessa.

For years, she struggled with being clingy in relationships: she'd constantly text, overthink every interaction with a man, and crave reassurance, even when things seemed to be going well.

The Loop:

"If I try hard enough, if I give more, do more, be more - he'll stay."

The Reset:

Once Vanessa explored her Love Style (which aligned with an anxious attachment style), everything started to make sense. Her need for closeness wasn't "too much"—it was a response to the uncertainty she had experienced in past relationships. With support, she stopped blaming herself and started building a new relationship with trust—first with herself, then with the partners she chose.

Key Takeaways:

- The stories we inherit from our families shape our beliefs about love, often unconsciously.

- Emotional distance can act as both a survival tool and a barrier to connection.

- Breaking free from these patterns requires self-reflection, vulnerability, and support.

Reflection Exercise:

- Reflect on a phrase about love you inherited from your family (e.g., "Ah suh dem stay" or "Men will be men"). Write about how it has influenced your relationships.

- Which attachment style resonates with you most right now? How does it connect to what you saw growing up and in your past relationships?

- Write down one small step you can take to let go of patterns or beliefs so you can create a new narrative.

Think about something you're ready to release, like overexplaining yourself or holding on too tightly out of fear.

Remember Vanessa? Once she understood her Love Style, she realized her need for closeness wasn't the problem, it was how she was seeking safety. By working together, she started to shift that. Her reset began with one small step: accepting that she was enough.

What might your first step be?

In Phase 4, I'll walk you through Love Styles, a lens for understanding how you date, how you connect, and what gets in the way. It's about recognizing your natural approach to love so you can make choices that truly support the relationship you want.

Take the Dating Reset Quiz now to discover your Love Style or go to www.NadiaEdwards.com/quiz

But first, up next in Phase 2, we'll be looking at how to clarify your core values and use them as a compass for connection.

CHAPTER 3:

PHASE 2:
ALIGNMENT

"I will not shrink to fit into spaces I've outgrown. I make space for what fits the life I'm creating." — Alex Elle

CHAPTER 4: RECONNECTING WITH YOURSELF

Finding the Real You

After years of chasing love, healing heartbreak, and carrying the weight of an emotional pile that wasn't serving me, I realized something: I had lost touch with myself.

It wasn't intentional. Life has a way of pulling us in so many directions—careers, families, responsibilities—that we don't always notice when we start to drift away from who we are. Add to that the experiences and expectations I'd been carrying since childhood, and it's no wonder I felt disconnected.

But here's the thing about losing yourself: You can always find your way back.

The Year of Rediscovery

I called it "The Year of Nadia." It was my personal dating sabbatical, a year where I hit pause on searching for love and focused entirely on reconnecting with myself.

At first, the idea of taking a break felt strange. I had spent so many years thinking that every date, every swipe, and every relationship might be "The One". I worried: *What if I take a year off and miss my chance? What if I end up alone forever?*

But as I reflected on the patterns and the emotional pile I'd been ignoring, I realized something: I couldn't keep running on autopilot. The kind of love I wanted required me to pause, reflect, and redefine.

During that year, I gave myself permission to rediscover the parts of me I had ignored or forgotten. I leaned into new interests, picked up hobbies I'd abandoned, and started paying attention to the things that brought me joy.

For the first time in years, I asked myself questions that were long overdue:

- Who am I?

- What lights me up and brings me joy?

- What kind of love do I want to experience?

- What does a truly fulfilling partnership look like for me?

The Power of Reflection

Reflection became a cornerstone of my rediscovery process. Every day, I'd journal my thoughts without judgment. Some days, the words came in a flood. Other days, I'd stare at a blank page, unsure of where to start.

But as the weeks turned into months, common themes began to emerge. I started to notice the beliefs I had been carrying—beliefs about myself, about love, about men, and about what I desired.

And I began to challenge them.

For example, I realized I had been measuring the success (often defined by length) of a relationship as though it reflected on my choices or judgment. I realized that if a relationship ended, it wasn't because I wasn't enough—I had always believed in my value. And it wasn't a sign that I had failed; it was an opportunity to hone in more clearly on exactly what I wanted.

Through journaling and reflection, I began to see relationships not as markers of success or failure, but as experiences that either aligned—or didn't align—with who I was and what I needed. My worth was never tied to a partner or a relationship—it had always been mine, unshakable and whole.

The truth is, reflection isn't always comfortable. Sometimes, I'd write things that made me cringe or feel exposed. But growth doesn't come from hiding. It comes from curiosity, from asking questions, like, "What if I try to see this differently?" and "Have my mindset and choices been serving me or not?"

The Shift from External to Internal

As I began reconnecting with myself, I noticed a shift. My focus moved away from what I wanted in a partner to how I wanted to feel in a relationship.

I no longer thought I needed someone to complete me; now I wanted someone to complement me.

I stopped looking for a savior or someone to fit into a fantasy. I was ready for a partner who could meet me as I was—fully, authentically, and without pretense.

I wanted a partner who was self-aware and ready to create a shared future, not just share a moment.

This shift also helped me understand the difference between the rush of being "in love," all those butterflies and brain chemicals, and building real love: a bond that's mutual, lasting, and deeply fulfilling.

And perhaps the biggest change of all? I no longer expected a partner to bring me happiness. I knew that was my job. A harmonious, loving relationship is the icing on the cake of a life I already love.

Because I bake my own cake.

This wasn't just empowering—it was liberating. It gave me the freedom to approach love without fear or desperation.

Practical Steps for Reconnecting with Yourself

If you're feeling disconnected from who you are, here are some steps to take:

1. **Take a Step Back**: Give yourself permission to reclaim your energy. That might mean a full dating sabbatical, like I did, or simply carving out intentional time for you—no apps, no "shoulds," just space to reconnect with who you are and what brings you joy. (And yes, that includes guilt-free Me Days on your calendar.)

2. **Revisit and Revive Your Joy**: Sometimes the best way to reconnect with yourself is to do things that light you up. These aren't just hobbies—they're pathways to remembering who you are outside of relationships. Try:
   - Joining a golf clinic or women's league
   - Signing up for a ballroom dance or salsa class
   - Booking a solo wellness retreat (a weekend counts)
   - Attending live music, art shows, or cultural events solo or with friends
   - Taking a cooking class and learning something new (just for the

fun of it)

- Reconnecting with a creative outlet—like painting, photography, music, or journaling
- Joining a walking group or outdoor adventure club
- Volunteering for a cause that matters to you
- Hosting an intimate dinner party for your inner circle.

3. **Show Yourself Compassion**: Reconnecting with yourself isn't about fixing what's broken, it's about remembering what's always been there. Give yourself grace.

Reclaiming Your Power

The path to reconnecting with yourself isn't about perfection, it's about presence.

It's about showing up for yourself in ways you never have before and recognizing that *you are your own greatest love story.*

Key Takeaways:

- Taking time to reconnect with yourself is essential for building aligned love.

- Reclaiming your power starts with knowing who you are and what you truly want.

- Doing what lights you up is an essential way to making yourself and your own happiness a priority.

Reflection Exercise:

- Write down three moments in your life when you felt most like yourself. What were you doing? Who were you with? Where were you? How did you feel?

- Choose 1-3 things you've neglected or have been curious about and do them today, this week, or this month.

- Based on what you've remembered and reclaimed, what matters most to you right now? Capture that in one clear sentence, and let it guide your next move.

In the next chapter, I'll share how you can redefine what love looks like so you can approach dating with more clarity and intention.

CHAPTER 4:

CHAPTER 5:
THE POWER OF LIVING ALIGNED LOVE

The Role of Values in Love

Have you ever looked back at a past relationship and thought, "What did I even see in him? How did I miss the signs that our values and goals were so different?"

This realization often comes too late, after heartbreak has already set in. But the truth is, alignment—or the lack of it—can make or break a relationship.

Your personal core values aren't just a list of traits or qualities; they're the foundation of who you are. They guide your decisions, your priorities, and the kind of life you want to enjoy living.

For years, I didn't give much thought to my values. I thought love was about finding someone who checked all the boxes: attractive, charming, successful. But even when I found men who fit that description, it always fell apart.

It wasn't until I started to *define my personal core values* that I realized that I had been prioritizing superficial qualities over deeper alignment.

Defining Your Core Values

Your core values are the principles and beliefs that guide your life. They reflect what matters most to you—whether it's honesty, family, fitness, creativity, personal growth, culture, politics, religion, or something else entirely.

In a relationship, *values alignment* means that both partners share similar priorities and beliefs about what's important. It doesn't mean you have to agree on everything, but your significant values should match each other.

Here are some examples:

- If you deeply value adventure and travel, you might struggle in a relationship with someone who values staying at home and sticking to the same routine.

- Someone who highly values family, wants children and grandchildren, and is willing to be a caregiver to their parents is not a great fit for someone who doesn't want all that responsibility.

- A person who reads the Bible, Talmud, or Koran daily and is devoted to daily prayer and frequent church or temple visits is not going to be comfortable with an atheist, agnostic, shaman, pagan, or "Love is my religion" type.

- If your partner takes fifteen supplements, makes healthy smoothies, eats organic or vegetarian only, doesn't drink or smoke, and you love fast food, frozen convenience meals, a couple of margaritas and smoke a pack of cigarettes every day, this is an argument waiting to happen or at the very least, eyes rolling.

It's not that one set of values is better than the other—they're just different. And without alignment, those differences can and will create tension over time because each of you will be wishing, even if it's not conscious, that the other person would be more like you, and you'll resent them wanting you to change you in ways that you don't feel need changing. And let me tell you, I don't care how good-looking they are or how good the sex is: If you don't share common core values, it's not going to work.

How to Define Your Core Values

Before you can apply this to dating, you need to be super clear about your own core values. Defining your core values is a vital process of self-discovery, for love and for life.

It requires you to look inward and ask yourself what truly matters to you at this point in your life—not what you've been told should matter, but what genuinely resonates with your heart and your vision of life and love.

I guide my clients through four values categories when helping them clarify their core ones. These categories offer a helpful starting point as you reflect on what matters most to you now:

1. **Emotional** – These speak to how you want to feel in a relationship and what you need emotionally to feel secure and connected.

2. **Practical** – These are about how someone moves through daily life.

3. **Lifestyle** – These focus on the rhythm and priorities of your life outside the relationship.

4. **Relational** – These get to the heart of how you want to relate and communicate with your partner.

Start by exploring the values that matter most to you across each category. Don't worry about narrowing them down just yet, this is about expanding your perspective. Thinking in categories helps you consider areas you may have overlooked, like how you want to feel emotionally, what kind of lifestyle supports you, how you relate in partnership, and the practical values that keep you grounded. These aren't just abstract ideas—they're clues to the kind of love and life you're ready to build.

Behind The Shift: Keisha Thought Shared Faith Was Enough

Let me tell you about Keisha, a client who was struggling to find a partner even though she was meeting men. On paper, she was clear about what she wanted: a man of God. In fact, religion was the only value on her list. She believed that shared faith would be enough, that if their faith matched, everything else would fall into place.

But during our work together, we walked through the values categories I use with all my clients, and it was like a lightbulb turned on.

- Physical health and wellness? That mattered.

- Quality time? Absolutely.

- Financial responsibility? Yes.

- Emotional safety? Definitely.

She realized she had never considered these other areas and that they were just as essential to building the kind of relationship she truly wanted. Faith was still important, but it wasn't the whole picture. Exploring the full range of values helped Keisha see that love requires more than spiritual compatibility. It requires alignment across the life she was actively living, not just the one she was hoping for.

When you group your values into categories, you'll see a more complete picture of what makes love feel good and what helps it last.

Here's an example of how your values might break down across the categories:

Emotional

These are about how you want to feel in a relationship and what you need emotionally to thrive.

- Trust
- Emotional safety
- Vulnerability
- Feeling seen and heard
- Empathy
- Respect

Practical

The everyday stuff that makes a relationship sustainable and helps life flow.

- Financial responsibility
- Physical health and wellness
- Cleanliness and organization

- Ambition
- Reliability
- Shared responsibility for home and life tasks.

Lifestyle

How you want to live and move through the world.

- Family relationships and closeness
- Travel and exploration
- Personal growth
- Cultural experiences (museums, music, food)
- Intellectual stimulation
- Beautiful home or aesthetic environments.

Relational

What love looks like in action and how connection is nurtured.

- Clear, open communication
- Affection, physical touch, sexual intimacy
- Monogamy or Ethical Non-Monogamy (ENM)
- Emotional availability
- Playfulness and humor
- Healthy conflict resolution and repair

This isn't about limiting your choices or forcing yourself to choose just a few things. It's about expanding your lens and getting clear on the full range of values that matter to you.

How to Self-Assess Your Values

1. **Review Your Life**: Think about the moments when you felt happiest and most fulfilled. What values were present in those moments? Now consider the times when you felt most disconnected or dissatisfied. What values were missing?

2. **Identify Themes**: Look for patterns in your reflections. For example, if you felt happiest when helping others, generosity or service might be a core value. If you felt most dissatisfied when someone lied to you, honesty is a priority.

3. **Create a List Across Categories**: Using the Emotional, Practical, Lifestyle, and Relational values categories as your guide, jot down values that feel most important to you.

4. **Test Your Values**: Think about how these values show up in your daily life. Are they truly guiding your decisions, or are they aspirational?

Once you've identified these, it's time to translate them into something practical: *The Alignment List.* This is your guide that will help you connect your values to specific, tangible qualities or behaviors you're seeking in a partner.

This list will help you move beyond abstract ideas so you can focus on recognizing alignment in real, demonstrated actions. For instance, if one of your core values is emotional safety, The Alignment List might include traits like "shares their feelings openly," "takes accountability during conflict," or "follows through on what they say."

If you value adventure, your list might include "plans spontaneous outings," "loves to explore new places," or "is open to trying new things together."

These are the real-life expressions of your values and when you see them show up in his behavior, you'll know you're not just clicking, you're aligning.

Living in Alignment

Living in alignment with your values isn't just about knowing what matters to you; it's about letting them guide how you show up in life and love.

For years, I wasn't living aligned love. I showed up with a version of myself that I thought would be "good enough" for a partner, often compromising my values to fit what he wanted. And every time I did that, it chipped away at my authenticity, and I felt unseen.

Behind the Shift: Monique Believed Her Success Pushed Men Away

Monique used to tone down her career drive on dates because she feared it drove men away. She wouldn't talk about her wins or future goals, thinking it might make her seem "too much." But in doing so, she kept ending up with partners who didn't celebrate her success, or worse, felt like they were in competition with her. Without realizing it, she was facilitating this misalignment by shrinking herself from the start.

The Loop:

"If I dim my light a little, I'll be more appealing to men."

The Reset:

Once Monique explored her full set of core values and started building The Alignment List, she realized her ambition and intelligence wasn't something to downplay; it was something to honor. She started showing up fully and unapologetically, knowing the right partner wouldn't be intimidated by her drive—he'd be drawn to it.

When you live aligned love, you don't have to shrink yourself or pretend to be someone you're not. You create space for the right person to connect with the real you. You allow yourself to be fully seen, heard, celebrated, and treasured for all of who you truly are.

The Challenges and Rewards of Aligned Love

The reality is, even alignment of core values doesn't guarantee that a relationship will be free of challenges. Every partnership encounters its share of conflicts and complexities. But alignment provides a strong foundation for navigating those challenges with intention and resilience, and it means that you are much more likely to be moving in a similar direction together, rather than drift apart as many couples do.

When you and your partner share values, you're better equipped to approach disagreements as a team, rather than adversaries. You make thoughtful decisions together and foster a sense of mutual support as you grow individually and as a couple.

When I finally found a partner who shared my values, love felt easier—like we are building something together rather than trying to force a connection that didn't align. The effort was still there, but it was a team effort in the same direction, with a shared vision guiding us forward.

Practical Steps for Living Aligned Love

1. **Check in With Your Values Regularly**: As you evolve, your values may shift, and that's ok. Take time to reassess what matters most to you and how it's showing up in your relationships.

2. **Be Honest from the Start**: Transparently share not only your personality but your values early in a relationship. This helps ensure you build a connection on a solid, meaningful foundation.

3. **Resist the Temptation to Overlook Misalignment**: Pay attention to signs of misalignment, even when they're subtle. These might feel familiar or comfortable, and your mind can try to trick you to rationalize them away or look only at the "the good stuff." Use The Alignment List as a guide to evaluate whether the connection aligns with your values so you can tell if this person can truly fulfill you and support the love you desire.

4. **Walk Away**: If a connection doesn't honor who you are, trust yourself to let it go. Walking away is an act of self-respect and courage. By releasing what is not aligned, you invite a partnership rooted in authenticity and mutual respect.

The Joy of Aligned Love

Living aligned love is a powerful experience. It's not just about finding the right partner; it's about becoming the best version of yourself and building a relationship that reflects your truest desires.

Aligned love doesn't happen by accident. It's a choice, a series of choices, really—that you both make every day. And when you choose to live authentically and honor your values, you create the kind of love that lasts and supports you both as you grow over the years.

Key Takeaways:

- Core values are your foundation. They define who you are and guide your priorities in life and love.

- Alignment is key to lasting love. Shared values create a strong foundation for navigating challenges and fostering growth as a couple.

- The Alignment List is your guide. It helps you move beyond abstract ideas and evaluate potential partners based on real, tangible behaviors.

- Authenticity attracts and nurtures aligned love. Showing up as your true self creates space for meaningful and fulfilling connections.

- Living aligned love is a choice. It requires daily decisions that honor your values and create the kind of love that feels deeply fulfilling.

Reflection Exercise:

Take a moment to consider your journey toward aligned love.

- Review The Alignment List. Are there any values or traits you want to refine or add based on what you've learned so far?

- Think about a recent relationship or interaction. Did it align with your core values? If not, what changes could you make in the future to honor your alignment?

- Write down one small step you can take this week to show up more authentically in a relationship or interaction.

You've been making amazing progress by coming this far, getting clear on your values and identifying what truly matters.

Next up, we're going to look at how you invest your most valuable resource: **your time**.

CHAPTER 5:

PHASE 3:
TIME

"What you water will grow."

— Thich Nhat Hanh

CHAPTER 6:
THE DATING SABBATICAL

The Dating Sabbatical and Self-Reflection

Taking a dating sabbatical may seem counterintuitive in a world that values action and achievement. But after years of dating and heartbreak, I realized I needed to pause—not as an act of defeat, but as an act of empowerment. I needed time to rediscover myself, free from the pressure of trying to find "The One."

During "The Year of Nadia," I focused on healing, silencing the negative self-talk, and embracing gratitude for the life I had. My mission was clear: to recalibrate my internal compass by determining:

What did I want love to look like for me?

What did I want to feel in a partnership?

As a single mother, this decision wasn't just for me—it was for my son, too. I saw this as a chance to break the cycle of viewing love as a duty or something to simply endure. I wanted him to see what an aligned and healthy romantic relationship could look like—one rooted in mutual respect, connection, and joy. Growing up, I didn't have that example, but I was determined to be it for him.

This sabbatical wasn't about retreating from life—it was about giving myself room to grow. I treated it like a personal growth project, diving into books about dating, love, and self-development. I learned to communicate my needs clearly instead of expecting a man to figure them out.

Before this sabbatical, I used to "recolor" any red flags into yellow or even green ones, convincing myself that things would improve. But I came to understand that love isn't hard—it's our attachment styles, past experiences, and societal norms that make it feel that way. At its core, love is simple.

And during that year, I asked myself this one question that changed everything:

What do I need to see and feel to know that he truly loves me for the real me?

It wasn't just about waiting to be chosen anymore. It was about seeking actions that demonstrated alignment and authenticity so that I did the choosing. I wasn't looking for perfection, but for someone who could love me for who I really was—the messy, growing, sometimes indecisive version of me as well as the smart, creative, confident woman I had become. I wasn't going to shrink or minimize myself to protect someone else's ego. I wanted a partner who saw, chose, and celebrated all of me.

This process gave me the clarity to recognize alignment and built my inner courage to walk away if it wasn't there.

And when I finally returned to dating, I approached it with intention, purpose, and a deeper understanding of what I truly desired.

Why Pause?

For me, the decision to take a sabbatical was transformative. But I know pausing can feel counterintuitive, especially in a world that tells us to: "Keep putting yourself out there" and "It's a numbers game."

If you're wondering whether a dating sabbatical might be right for you, ask yourself:

- Are you dating out of habit or intention?

- Do you feel like you're chasing something instead of creating space for it to align with you?

Benefits of the Dating Sabbatical

By stepping back, you give yourself the opportunity to:

1. **Rebuild Self-Love**: Pour into yourself with care, patience, and honesty. This is about choosing yourself every day, not just when you're single.

2. **Reclaim Balance**: Focus on the areas of your life that bring joy and fulfillment—your health, friendships, passions, and purpose—so you step into your next relationship from a place of strength, not scarcity.

3. **Gain Clarity**: Reflect on what kind of partnership actually supports the life you're building. With this kind of awareness, you're not just dating—you're deciding.

Most importantly, pausing allows you to reconnect with your worth and build the courage to move forward intentionally, even when fear is still present.

What My Sabbatical Looked Like

The sabbatical wasn't just about avoiding dating apps or declining invitations; it was about shifting my focus entirely. I stopped looking outward and started looking inward.

I spent that year journaling, meditating, and working with a dating coach to unpack the beliefs and behaviors that had been holding me back. I returned to hobbies I had neglected, like going to art museums and traveling, and invested in the friendships and family relationships that nourished me.

Most importantly, I gave myself permission to let go of the pressure to "find a husband." Instead, I focused on becoming someone I loved being with.

That's not to say fear didn't creep in. I worried: *What if I'm doing this all wrong? What if I spend a year rediscovering myself and still don't find love?*

But I made a choice: I would move forward with the fear. I even named my fear: "Fitzroy."

Why Fitzroy? I don't know, it just fit. It made the fear feel like less of a shadowy monster and more like that dramatic uncle who always has something to say but doesn't know what he's talking about.

Fitzroy would show up right before a date, arms crossed and full of opinions:

Fitzroy: "You really think someone's going to love this version of you? Please. You're too much. And not enough. At the same time."

Me: (deep breath) "Thanks for your concern, Fitzroy. But we've been through this. I'm not waiting for your approval to live my life."

Naming my fear gave me a way to recognize it without letting it run the show. Fitzroy could ride along in the backseat but he wasn't allowed to drive. And when he got too loud? I reminded him he was one wrong word away from being tossed in the trunk.

Fear of Missing Out (FOMO)

At first, the idea of taking a year off scared me. *What if I miss my chance to meet the right man? What if I am already too old, and taking a pause only makes it harder to find love?*

But here's what I discovered: Pausing doesn't mean you're falling behind. It's actually a way to fast-track your journey toward the love you truly deserve.

By giving myself the time and space to reflect, I became intentional about how I approached love. No more swiping out of boredom, going on dates just to get back out there, or trying to fill a void.

Instead, I was learning to align my actions with my values, and preparing myself for a connection that felt authentic, fulfilling, and resonant with my vision for love.

What I Learned from the Pause

That year of intentional stillness gave me clarity I didn't even know I needed. Here's what I discovered:

1. **I Am Whole on My Own**: I didn't need a relationship to complete my life—I was already enough.

2. **Clarity Comes with Stillness**: When I stopped chasing, everything became clearer.

3. **Love Is Not a Race**: Taking time for myself didn't delay love; it

prepared me for it.

4. **Fear Doesn't Have to Stop You**: I realized I didn't need to be fearless to take action. I just had to move forward anyway.

5. **I Am Lovable as I Am**. I don't have to be perfectly healed to be ready for real love with the right person.

Is a Dating Sabbatical Right for You?

A dating sabbatical isn't for everyone, and it doesn't have to be a year-long commitment. The goal isn't about time, it's about intention. If you feel stuck, overwhelmed, or disconnected from yourself, a pause might be exactly what you need.

Give yourself permission to set a time frame, maybe it's a few weeks, a couple of months, or even a season. Mark it on your calendar and treat it with the same intention you'd bring to a major life goal.

When that time is up, check in with yourself:
- How are you?
- Have your values and desires become clearer?
- Does the idea of dating feel expansive or still draining?

You don't need to have it all figured out to return to dating. But when your curiosity starts to outweigh your fear, when you begin to feel open to possibility again, that's your sign. And if you don't feel that readiness yet, you can extend your sabbatical for whatever time frame feels right.

As my client Candice put it:

"I had an amazing time on a girls' trip, but when I looked around and saw couples enjoying each other at the resort together, something hit me. I realized: *I want that, too.* Not just travel, but to share these experiences with the man I love. That moment gave me the nudge I needed to put myself back into dating so I can have that experience, too."

She wasn't chasing a fantasy. She was honoring a desire. And that kind of clarity? That's exactly what a dating sabbatical is meant to create.

Let your return be authentic, intentional, and led by what truly feels right for you.

Key Takeaways:

- A dating sabbatical is a powerful way to break patterns, gain clarity, and reconnect with yourself.

- Taking intentional time to pause doesn't mean falling behind—it prepares you for aligned love.

- Pausing allows you to rediscover your worth, reconnect with your values, and approach dating with a renewed sense of purpose and empowerment.

Reflection Exercise:

- Think about your past and current dating habits. Are they intentional or reactive? Write down one pattern or belief that you want to shift.

- Imagine taking a dating sabbatical. How long might you like your pause to be? (perhaps three, six, nine, or twelve months) What would you focus on during that time? List three areas of personal growth or discovery.

- Identify one fear you have about pausing or about moving forward. Write one action step you can take to move with that fear.

In the next chapter, we'll dive deeper into how pacing yourself can be a game changer as you move forward.

CHAPTER 6:

CHAPTER 7:
PATIENCE AND PERSPECTIVE

The Value of Intentional Pacing

In midlife, dating isn't about racing to find "The One." For many women, the challenge at this stage of life is not the pressure to hurry to settle down, or a biological clock ticking—it's the temptation to believe too soon that he might be the right one for you.

When you approach dating with patience and intention, you create the time and space to evaluate a man's actions, observe his alignment with your values, and ensure the connection is right before investing emotionally.

Intentional pacing isn't about passivity; it's about slowing down with purpose. It's about giving yourself permission to consider, observe, and trust the process, knowing that each step you take brings you closer to the aligned love you desire.

Dating Multiple Men at Once

One of the most impactful ways I practiced intentional pacing was by dating multiple men at once.

For years, I had fallen into the trap of fixating on one man too quickly, getting emotionally attached before I had the clarity to assess whether the connection was actually aligned. I would fill in the blanks with potential and hold on too long, hoping it would turn into something real. So when my dating coach encouraged me to date multiple men at the same time, my first reaction was: "Nah, that's not for me. I'm a one-man woman."

But I was also ready to try something different. And I quickly realized this wasn't about "playing the field" or keeping a roster. It was about keeping myself emotionally aloof long enough to actually observe the man in front of me.

Here's why this strategy worked for me:

• It helped me stay emotionally balanced and prevented premature commitment. I didn't rush to make a man "The One" before I had enough information.

• It gave me perspective. By experiencing different interactions, I could better see what truly felt good and what didn't.

• It reinforced abundance. I stopped obsessing over who was texting back and started trusting that there were plenty of great men out there who also wanted love.

And here's what it didn't mean:

It didn't mean I was sleeping with multiple men. In fact, I recommend no sex at all while dating multiple men.

That's not about shame, it's about science. Sexual intimacy releases chemicals like oxytocin and dopamine in a woman's brain, which can create a false sense of connection, attachment, or trust before real compatibility has been established. It clouds judgment. And when you're trying to date with clarity? That's the last thing you want.

Behind the Shift: Tasha Didn't Want Another Situationship

One of my clients, Tasha, is smart, beautiful, and successful—the kind of woman people assume is in a relationship. But despite all she had going for her, she kept ending up in situationships that left her feeling confused and disappointed.

She used to tell herself, "It's just sex. It doesn't mean anything." But after each encounter, she'd find herself catching feelings and expecting the man to feel the same way, simply because they'd been physically intimate. Most of the time, he didn't. And she'd be left wondering what went wrong. And even worse, feeling unworthy and unlovable.

Once she understood the emotional toll sex was taking, and how it blurred her vision and made her stay longer than she should, she decided to try something new. She committed to a dating reset. No sex. No over-investing. No rushing.

When I introduced Tasha to the technique of dating multiple men without sexual intimacy, everything shifted. She slowed down. She stopped overcommitting to men who didn't show up in the ways that mattered. She dated with her eyes open and her heart protected, asking better questions and taking her time. She started choosing, instead of waiting to be chosen.

That's when the shift happened. She could finally see who was consistent, who followed through, and who was just coasting on chemistry. For the first time, she felt in control because she was choosing from a place of clarity, not longing.

Dating with an abundance mindset doesn't require being emotionally or physically available to every man; it requires being available to yourself first.

So, no, dating multiple men isn't about playing games. It's about giving yourself permission to take your time, get curious, and be selective—not desperate.

You're allowed to explore. You're allowed to stay open. And you're allowed to change your mind.

When you pace yourself intentionally, you give yourself the gift of perspective and that's one of the most underrated superpowers in dating.

Think about your own dating experiences:

- Have you ever overcommitted emotionally too soon?

- How might exploring multiple connections help you gain clarity about what you truly want?

How to Date Multiple Men, with Integrity

If you're curious about trying this approach, here are some tips to navigate it with clarity and integrity:

- **Be Honest**: Transparency is key. Let each person know you're exploring connections and being intentional in your dating journey. Honesty builds trust and keeps things respectful. This isn't the same as practicing ethical non-monogamy, which is a relationship structure where people openly have multiple romantic or sexual partners.

- **Reflect Often**: After each date or interaction, take time to assess. How did you feel? Did the connection align with your values? (Refer to your Alignment List.) What did you learn about yourself or your needs? I recommend that you do this in writing, in your journal (paper or electronic). You can also process these dating experiences and observations with a trusted friend, family member, coach or therapist. This will help you see and remember your learnings over time.

This approach isn't for everyone, and that's okay. But for me, and many of the women I've helped, it's been a game-changer.

Client Story: Nia Dates Multiple Men Without Guilt

After a painful breakup, Nia, a high-achieving, beautiful woman in her 40s, and a total social ninja, came to me feeling raw and unsure.

"I even cut off all my hair," she told me. "I thought maybe starting fresh on the outside would help numb the pain I was carrying on the inside."

Attracting men had never been her problem. But this time, she wasn't looking for attention; she was looking for alignment.

She was tired of jumping in too quickly and hoping for the best. She wanted clarity, ease, and permission to do things differently.

One of the biggest shifts we worked on was giving herself full permission to date multiple men without guilt, not to play games, but to truly enjoy the process while figuring out who was genuinely aligned with her vision for partnership.

She also began sharing her intentions clearly and early. On first and second dates, Nia let men know up front: "I'm actively dating because I'm looking for a life partner."

That one sentence became a powerful filter. It opened the door for honesty, cut through mixed signals, and helped her stay rooted in her purpose.

As Nia put it: "For the first time, I'm not chasing love. I'm choosing it. I'm finally enjoying dating because I know what to look for and how to ask meaningful questions without it feeling like an interrogation."

She stopped second-guessing herself. She stopped waiting for permission. And she started dating with joy, confidence, and full ownership of what she wanted and deserved.

Trusting the Timing of Your Journey

Practicing patience in dating means trusting that everything is unfolding at the right time. It means letting go of the pressure to rush, and instead welcoming opportunities to grow, learn, and connect along the way.

At times, I worried I was moving too slowly. But as I practiced patience, I realized that aligned love isn't something you rush into, it's something you build with care and intention.

Depending on your Love Style, you might approach commitment in different ways.

If you identify with The Over-Giver (which often maps to an anxious attachment style), you might feel tempted to jump in quickly, hoping exclusivity will create security.

On the flip side, if you lean more toward The Cautious Skeptic (which aligns with avoidant tendencies), you might keep things casual for too long as a way to protect yourself from vulnerability.

Neither one is wrong but both benefit from self-awareness and intentional pacing.

The Alignment List can help you spot the difference between potential and alignment. When a man *consistently* shows up in ways that match your values, not just once, but over time, that's your cue to consider going deeper.

Trusting the timing of your journey means making space to evaluate, not just emotionally react.

When you date with patience, you're not just hoping for love to happen. You're creating the conditions for it to thrive.

Key Takeaways:

- Intentional pacing allows you to evaluate connections, gain clarity, and avoid rushing into misaligned relationships.

- Dating multiple men at once can be a powerful strategy for maintaining emotional balance, exploring options, and staying grounded in your values.

- Trusting the timing of your journey means letting go of external pressures and embracing the process as it unfolds.

Reflection Exercise:

- **Reflect on Your Current Approach**: Take a moment to evaluate how you've been approaching dating. Are you rushing into relationships, or are you taking the time to understand alignment? Identify habits that might be holding you back.

- **Explore Multiple Connections**: If it feels right for you, consider dating multiple men at once to explore options without overcommitting emotionally too soon.

- **Savor the Journey**: Slow down and focus on enjoying the dating process rather than rushing toward a specific outcome. Journal after each date, take intentional pauses to reflect, and let yourself fully experience the journey.

In Chapter 8, you'll explore what it really means to prioritize love.

CHAPTER 8:
MAKING ROOM FOR LOVE

Why Balance Matters

When we're younger, in the pursuit of love, it's easy to let other areas of your life take a back seat. But for many women in midlife, the opposite is true: Love becomes an afterthought, squeezed into the tiny gaps between work, family, exercise, and everything else on the to-do list.

Here's the truth: Aligned love doesn't just happen. It requires intentional effort. It's not about hoping you'll meet the right person when the stars align or when your schedule magically clears up. It's about choosing to make love a priority in your life, just as you would any other important goal.

For years, I treated dating like an afterthought. I went on dates when I "had time," squeezing them in between everything else. But when I started prioritizing love, when I put dating on my calendar and treated it like the meaningful commitment it was—everything shifted.

Balancing Independence and Connection

One of the biggest challenges in creating balanced love is maintaining your independence while fostering meaningful connection.

For me, this meant learning how to integrate love into my life without losing myself in the process. It meant continuing to pursue my goals, nurture my friendships, and invest in my passions while making time for dating.

Here's how you can balance independence and connection:

1. **Set Clear Boundaries**: Boundaries protect your time, energy, and identity. They ensure you're not overextending yourself for a relationship.

2. **Communicate Honestly**: Talk to your partner or potential partners about your priorities and how you're working to integrate love into your life in a way that's balanced, sustainable, and healthy.

3. **Keep Your Passions Alive**: Don't give up the things that make you feel alive and fulfilled. Stop waiting for your partner to arrive in order to do the things you want to do, and go to the places you want to go. The right partner will support and celebrate your independence, and the more passionately alive you are when you find each other, the more well-rounded and happy a person you bring into your partnership.

Creating Space for Love

Making room for love isn't just about freeing up time—it's about clearing out the emotional pile that's crowding your ability to connect.

One of the simplest but most powerful things I did was block off time on my calendar every single week for dating. After work, I was already dressed and in that "out in the world" energy, so I'd plan to meet someone for a date. If there wasn't a man I was interested in or actively chatting with, I didn't cancel. I took myself out. Whether it was dinner, a museum, or just sitting at the bar with a book and a glass of wine, I stayed consistent and honored that time.

And here's the best part: Solo dates released the pressure. I wasn't showing up with first-date jitters. I was just enjoying my evening, being myself. And that energy? Magnetic. Men would approach me, and the conversation flowed because I was relaxed and unbothered. If there was interest, we'd stay in touch and make plans for a real date—no force, no performance.

This is a shift I guide a lot of women through. And here's another tip: Many are used to only going on dates on Friday or Saturday nights, those high-stakes, super couple-y evenings when restaurants are packed and expectations are high. But when they start scheduling dates during the week—Tuesday happy hours, Wednesday art shows, a Thursday cooking class, they begin to enjoy the process more. The pressure drops, the energy shifts, and it starts to feel like something they're doing for themselves, not just in hopes of finding "The One."

Aligned love doesn't just happen—it's built. And building it requires intentional space. Dating isn't just something to "squeeze in" when life slows down. It's the prerequisite for the relationship you say you want.

If you don't feel like you have time to date, how will you have time for a relationship or a life partner?

Creating space doesn't mean you have to overhaul your life. It means carving out time, on purpose, for connection, joy, and possibility.

Practical Steps for Building Balance

- **Block Off Time for Dating**: Schedule time for connection, whether it's meeting new people, nurturing existing relationships, or simply reflecting on what you want.

- **Protect Your Energy, Not Your Calendar**: Ask yourself if you're truly "too busy" to date or if staying busy has become a shield. Look for a weekly window of time you can reclaim and intentionally devote to love.

- **Honor Your Independence**: Maintain your hobbies, passions, and friendships while integrating love into your life. The right partner will complement, not compete with, your independence.

Key Takeaways:

- Balanced love requires intentional effort. Make dating a priority by putting it on your calendar.

- Clearing the emotional pile creates the space you need to approach love with openness and clarity.

- Prioritizing love doesn't mean losing yourself; it's about creating room for connection while maintaining independence.

Reflection Exercise:

- What does your current weekly schedule reveal about your priorities, and where can love fit in?

- Where can you expand your comfort zone by choosing different days or times to go out or meet new men?

- How can you remind yourself that prioritizing love is a powerful choice, not a passive hope?

You've started to make space for love in your life—on purpose. You've challenged the idea that you're "too busy" and created new rhythms that make room for connection. That's no small thing.

But even with that space, fear can still sneak in:

What if I get hurt again?

What if no one shows up?

What if I'm wasting my time?

In the next chapter, we'll explore what it means to shift out of fear and into intention.

PHASE 4:
INTENTION

"You're choosing someone who will share your energy, your body, your space, your time and even your finances. Heck yes, you should be picky."

— Nadia Edwards

CHAPTER 9:
MOVING FROM FEAR TO INTENTION

The Problem with Fear in Dating

Dating without clarity can feel like navigating a maze designed by fear. Fear of rejection, fear of repeating past mistakes, fear of not being enough—or too much.

All these fears can make you second-guess your decisions, hesitate when you want to move forward, or settle when deep down, you know you desire something else. Over time, fear can leave you avoiding dating altogether, unsure of how to begin again.

For years, fear guided my approach to dating. I wasn't reckless or careless... but I wasn't intentional either. Instead of clarity, I relied on hope—hoping that if I just kept trying, the right man would eventually show up.

I'd meet a man and hope for a spark, but nothing ever seemed to lead to the connection I truly wanted. It's easy to fall into patterns of reactive dating—choosing convenience, chemistry, or even a fear of being alone over clear intention.

What I didn't realize was that meaningful connections don't happen by chance. They're built with intention, and intention begins with alignment: alignment with your values, desires, and the kind of relationship you truly want.

Bringing The Alignment List into Dating

In Phase 2, you created your Alignment List—a reflection of your core values, non-negotiables, and the qualities you're seeking in a partner. This isn't just a one-time exercise; it's your organically evolving guide to dating with purpose and clarity.

The Alignment List helps you stay grounded in what truly matters, even when distractions or doubt arise. It's your compass, pointing you toward connections that align with your values and desires.

Here's how to use your Alignment List as a practical tool in your dating life:

- **Refer to It Often**: Before a date, review your list to center yourself on your values and intentions. Create questions that you can weave into a conversation.

- **Check for Alignment**: After a date or interaction, ask yourself: Does this person demonstrate the qualities I'm seeking? Does this connection reflect my values?

- **Stay True to Yourself**: If you feel tempted to overlook red flags or compromise on your needs, your list can help you course-correct and honor your boundaries.

What Is Dating with Intention?

Dating with intention means approaching every interaction—whether it's a swipe, a message, a phone or video conversation, or a date—with clarity about who you are, what you want, and how you want to show up.

It's not about following rigid rules or clinging to a checklist. Instead, it's about using tools like your Alignment List to shape your decisions while remaining open to authentic connection.

Here's what dating with intention can look like:

- **Clarity About Yourself**: Knowing your values, priorities, and what you're truly seeking in a partner.

- **Purposeful Actions**: Making choices that align with your goals, rather than acting out of fear, convenience, or impulse.

- **Open Communication**: Being honest about your intentions and values, even when it feels vulnerable.

The Shift from Fear to Intention

The shift from fear-based dating to intentional dating begins with reflection. You can't create clarity in connection until you've done the inner work to understand your patterns and have a vision for love.

When I started this process, I asked myself tough but necessary questions:

- *Why am I dating? Am I seeking connection, or am I trying to fill a void?*

- *What patterns have I been repeating, and how can I step out of them?*

- *How do I want to feel in a relationship? What kind of partner aligns with that vision?*

These questions helped me uncover the truth about what I truly wanted and just as importantly, what I didn't want.

Practical Steps for Creating Clarity

If you're ready to transition from fear and hesitation to intention and manifestation, here are actionable steps to guide you:

1. **Define Your Why**: Reflect on why you're dating. Are you seeking a life partner? Companionship? Personal growth? Your why is your

big-picture motivation, it's the deeper reason behind your desire for connection. Knowing your why provides focus and helps you navigate the dating world with clarity and purpose, especially when the journey feels uncertain or discouraging.

2. **Set Intentions, Not Goals**: While your "why" grounds you in the bigger purpose, your intentions guide how you want to move through the dating experience day-to-day. Think about what you hope to feel, explore, or create in this season of dating. Maybe you want to meet someone who shares your values. Maybe you want to reawaken your sexual self or explore emotional intimacy. Or maybe you just want to practice being seen, expressing your needs, or enjoying the moment without pressure. Intentions help shift your focus from "Is he The One?" to "Is this experience aligned with who I am and what I want more of?"

3. **Reflect After Every Interaction**: Every date or connection, whether it leads to something romantic or not, is valuable data. Take a moment to check in with yourself after each interaction:

- Did I feel like myself?
- Did this experience align with my values or stretch me in a healthy way?
- What did I notice about my patterns, preferences, or triggers

Reflection doesn't have to be heavy; it can be a five-minute voice note, a journal prompt, or a quick mental scan on the ride home. Over time, these check-ins help you build clarity, strengthen your gut intuition, and refine your dating experience with intention instead of reacting from fear or habit.

The Freedom of Intention

When you date with intention, you're not chasing love or molding yourself to fit someone else's vision. You're showing up authentically, anchored in clarity and purpose. This shift is freeing. It allows you to focus on what aligns with your values instead of forcing connections that don't feel right.

Dating with intention also means trusting the process. Some connections won't lead anywhere, but that doesn't mean you've failed or that there aren't any good men left. You're simply refining your understanding of what works and what doesn't.

Key Takeaways:

- Dating with intention means approaching every interaction with clarity, authenticity, and purpose.

- The Alignment List is your compass for staying grounded in your values and priorities.

- Intention creates freedom. You're no longer chasing connection; you're allowing it to unfold naturally.

Reflection Exercise:

Here are a few ways to personally connect with this chapter and bring more clarity into your dating life:

- **Review The Alignment List**. Revisit your list to ensure it aligns with your current actions and choices.

- **Clarify Your "Why."** Write down your intention for dating in this season of your life. What are you truly seeking beyond just "a relationship"? Why does it matter to you now? Let your answer anchor you when fear, doubt, or distractions pop up.

- **Set a Micro-Intention.** This could be scheduling a solo or partnered date with intention, journaling after an interaction, or practicing saying "No" to a connection that feels misaligned—even if it looks good on paper or other people think they're a fit for you.

In the next chapter, we'll dive into values-based dating so you can stop second-guessing and start choosing from a place of truth.

CHAPTER 10:
VALUES-BASED DATING

Why Values Matter in Dating

In dating, it's easy to get swept up in chemistry, charm, or the thrill of a budding relationship. But true compatibility goes deeper. What really matters is how much fun you have on a date and whether your values are in sync, so the relationship has the foundation to grow into something meaningful.

Values-based dating shifts your focus from surface-level attraction and short-term pleasure to deeper compatibility. It's about choosing partners whose core beliefs, priorities, and life goals align with yours.

Here's the truth: Love built on aligned values lasts, while love built on misalignment often leads to frustration and heartbreak.

Chemistry Is Never Enough

The popular Netflix reality show *The Later Daters* follows a group of singles navigating the complexities of dating later in life. Each participant brings a lifetime of experiences, values, and hopes to the process, making for an insightful look at dating in midlife.

One cast member, a woman in her 60s and three times divorced, stood out to me. Her situation felt so relatable not just to my own journey, but to the stories I hear from my clients. She had been working with a dating coach to refine her approach to dating, determined to break old patterns. But when her daughter selected a date for her, a man who was her "type," she couldn't resist. He was charming, attractive, confident, and their chemistry was undeniable.

On the show, it seemed like the perfect story. They walked off together, and viewers were left with the impression of a budding romance. But later, on social media, it was revealed that the relationship hadn't lasted. Despite the initial spark, their misaligned values and lifestyles made it unsustainable.

This story resonated deeply because it's one I've heard, seen—and lived—before. Chemistry can feel magical in the moment, like fireworks lighting up the night sky. But just like fireworks, it's fleeting.

Lasting love isn't built on the rush of attraction—it's built on the steady foundation of shared values.

The Problem with Misalignment

CHAPTER 10:

In one of my past relationships, I overlooked our differences because the chemistry was strong and he fit my "type." He was a C-suite executive in the financial world—ambitious, sharp, and always on the move. He worked long hours, loved adventure, and had that magnetic charm that drew people in. On paper, he looked ideal: successful, exciting, worldly.

But in reality, we were in two very different places.

He thrived on constant stimulation, big social scenes, and being surrounded by women who were drawn to powerful men like him. He was deeply committed to his career, which was the great love of his life at the time. And while I respected that, I was in a season where I was craving emotional intimacy and consistent one-on-one connection. I was more of a quiet-evenings, relax-on-the-beach kind of woman.

To make things more complicated, my girlfriends thought he was perfect. Because he checked all their boxes, so they couldn't understand why I wasn't head over heels. I felt this subtle pressure to make it work; He was the kind of man every woman was supposed to want. But the truth? He didn't check mine. I told myself I should be grateful, that I should just adjust my expectations and lifestyle. And for a while, I tried. But deep down, I knew I wasn't being honest with myself.

When I eventually expressed what I needed—more time, more presence, more depth—he couldn't meet me there. Not because he didn't care, but because he didn't have the capacity. And instead of feeling supported, I started to feel like I was asking for too much.

What I've come to realize is this: He wasn't a bad person. He just wasn't aligned with the kind of partnership I was ready for. And when values and timing don't line up, even the strongest connection won't be enough to sustain the relationship.

Love can't thrive when you're in two different seasons of life.

You're allowed to say no to what looks good if it doesn't feel good.

Recognizing Alignment Early

Values-based dating doesn't mean waiting months or years to discover whether someone is a good fit. You can often identify alignment (and misalignment) early by being intentional in how you approach dating and communication.

Here are some strategies for recognizing alignment early:

1. **Use Advanced Small Talk**: Move beyond basic small talk and explore topics that reveal someone's values, such as their priorities, goals, and views on relationships. Talk about your own core values, and tell stories that show you walking the talk.

2. **Observe Their Actions**: Pay attention to how they show up. Do their actions align with their words? Are they consistent and trustworthy?

3. **Be Honest About Your Intentions**: Share your values and what

you're looking for early on. This helps ensure you're on the same page from the start.

Think about your last few dates or relationships:

- Did you notice early signs of alignment or misalignment?

- How can you bring more intentionality into your next connection?

The Role of Non-Negotiables

Your non-negotiables are the foundation of values-based dating. They're the qualities or values you absolutely need in a partner for the relationship to thrive. Your "must haves."

And let me say this plainly: You're not too picky for having them.

You're choosing someone who will share your energy, your body, your home, your time, your finances, and your peace. **Heck yes, you should be picky**. This isn't about finding someone who just texts you back or keeps you company on weekends, this is about building a partnership that honors who you are and shares the vision you have for love.

Now, let's keep it real, some people around you (even the ones who love you) might not get it. They might tell you you're being too picky, and that can trigger self-doubt. You might start wondering if you're asking for too much.

But here's the truth: a man can seem like a great catch and still not be right *for you*.

Now, that doesn't mean fixating on whether he has a full head of hair or is at least six feet tall. Your non-negotiables should go deeper into how you want to feel in partnership, your lifestyle, and the values you're not willing to compromise on. **This isn't about having a checklist, it's about having a vision.**

For me, one non-negotiable was emotional availability. I knew I wanted a partner who could communicate openly and show up fully in the relationship. In the past, I had ignored this need, hoping that emotional distance would resolve itself over time. But when I made it a non-negotiable, I stopped wasting time on connections that couldn't meet me where I was.

You don't need to justify your standards. You just need to honor them

Here's how to define and honor your non-negotiables:

1. **Identify Them**: Reflect on what you absolutely need in a relationship. What values or qualities are essential to you? Write them down.

2. **Communicate Them**: Be upfront about your non-negotiables when the time is right. You don't need to list them on a first date or a dating app, or you can if that feels right to you, but clarity

early on will save both you and your potential partner time and heartache.

3. **Stick to Them**: It's tempting to compromise when chemistry is strong, or if you've been dating for a long time, but staying true to your non-negotiables makes sure you're building a relationship on solid ground.

The Pitfall of Assumption

One of the biggest pitfalls for later daters is assuming you already know who a man is without asking the right questions.

After years of experience, it's easy to rely on instinct, spotting familiar traits and filling in the blanks based on past relationships. You think, *I've seen this before. I know how this goes.*

But assumptions can be misleading. A man's surface-level qualities—his charm, career, looks, or shared interests—don't necessarily reveal his character, values, or emotional availability.

Real connection comes from curiosity.

You need to ask questions, listen without projecting, and allow someone to reveal themselves over time. Values-based dating means resisting the urge to define a man too quickly—whether positively or negatively—and instead, being open to discovering who he truly is. You learn this not only from how he responds to your questions, and what sorts of questions he asks you and seems curious about, but also his actions. His energy. Pay attention to patterns, too.

The Freedom of Alignment

When you date with your values in mind, it's less about proving yourself to someone else and more about discerning who complements your life. It's about confidently stepping into the dating world knowing you're already whole and seeking someone who aligns with the life you've built and the vision you have for your next phase in life.

Because values-based dating isn't just about finding the "perfect" partner—it's about creating a relationship where both people feel seen, valued, and respected. Together, you build a connection that mutually honors your authenticity and aligns with your vision for love.

Key Takeaways:

- Chemistry may feel magical, but lasting love requires shared values and alignment.

- Use advanced small talk to uncover his values and share yours.

- Honoring your non-negotiables ensures you're building a relationship on a foundation of alignment.

Reflection Exercise:

- **Name Your Non-Negotiables:** Write down three values that are essential to the kind of love you want to build. Why are they non-negotiable? What do they look like in action?

- **Master the Art of Advanced Small Talk**: Think of questions that you can weave naturally into a conversation. This way, you can gain meaningful insights without it feeling like an interrogation.

- **Look Back With Clarity:** Think of a time when chemistry clouded your judgment. What value was missing in that relationship and how will you spot that earlier next time?

In the next chapter, we'll explore what it looks like to bring your full, authentic self to the dating process and understand your Love Style.

CHAPTER 10:

CHAPTER 11:
THE EMPOWERED APPROACH

Dating in the Modern World

Modern dating often feels like a race, an endless push to keep up with trends, swipe on dating apps, update profiles, speed date, or treat finding love like a numbers game. But for many women in midlife, this approach is exhausting and feels disconnected from their true desires.

But what if dating didn't have to feel so frustrating?

What if, instead of seeking chemistry or surface-level attraction, you had a clear sense of what works for you - how you love, what you need, and what tends to throw you off balance?

That's what your Love Style reveals. It's not a label, it's a lens. One that helps you understand how you show up in love so you can connect and communicate from a place of clarity.

Discovering Your Love Style

Every woman brings her own energy, beliefs, and habits into dating. Over time, I started to notice common threads in how my clients were experiencing love: not just who they were drawn to, but how they expressed affection, responded to conflict, and defined connection. These patterns weren't random; they reflected something deeper.

That's where your Love Style comes in.

Your Love Style is the unique way you experience, express, and navigate love. It's shaped by your attachment patterns, dating behaviors, and emotional needs. It influences how you connect with others romantically, how you communicate affection, and what you need to feel secure and fulfilled in a relationship.

Understanding your Love Style is about recognizing your patterns, honoring your emotional needs, and dating in a way that reflects your truth, not your past. Once you have that clarity, you can begin to date with more ease, confidence, and connection.

The Dating Reset Method supports women who tend to fall into one of four Love Styles.

Let's take a look at each one:

1. The Over-Giver

You're the nurturer, the woman who leads with her heart and shows up with care, generosity, and emotional availability. You deeply value connection and will pour into your relationships, often giving the benefit of the doubt and doing the emotional heavy lifting.

The challenge? You sometimes prioritize others' needs over your own, holding onto relationships longer than you should. You may fear that pulling back or asking for more will cause someone to leave. But real connection doesn't require you to over-function; it requires reciprocity.

2. The Romantic Optimist

You're the hopeful believer, still open to love even after disappointment. You lead with curiosity, emotion, and a sense of possibility. You believe your person is out there and are willing to put yourself out there too.

The challenge? Your enthusiasm can lead to early emotional investment before someone has truly earned it. You may find yourself focusing on how much they like you instead of how aligned they actually are with you. Your hope is beautiful, just make sure it's paired with discernment.

3. The Cautious Skeptic

You're the realist: practical, independent, and grounded. You don't get swept up in fairy tales or chemistry alone. You approach dating with thoughtful intention, taking your time before letting someone in.

The challenge? Your independence can become a shield. You might keep people at a distance to avoid vulnerability or feel safer when you're the one in control. But intimacy requires trust, and that means allowing yourself to be seen.

4. The Independent Protector

You're the guarder of peace. You've done the self-work, built a life you love, and aren't willing to compromise your emotional well-being just to say you're in a relationship. You've likely been through emotionally demanding partnerships, and now, you're much more discerning.

The challenge? You may assume relationships will be draining, even when they're not. You've traded openness for safety, but love needs a little risk. You don't need to lower your standards. You just need to trust that you can honor your boundaries while still letting the right one in.

Curious about your Love Style?

Take the Dating Reset Quiz at www.NadiaEdwards.com/quiz to discover yours!

Let's look at how understanding your Love Style can create real change.

Behind the Shift: Nancy Let Her Fear Rush the Relationship

Nancy, in her late 50s, came to me feeling discouraged after years of dating that left her disappointed and emotionally drained. Despite being warm, open-hearted, and hopeful about love, she often found herself getting emotionally attached too quickly. She would invest in men she barely knew, driven by an underlying fear that love might pass her by if she didn't act fast.

Nancy resonated deeply with the Romantic Optimist Love Style. She craved deep, meaningful connection and felt most at ease in slower, more intentional environments. But her fear of missing out (FOMO) would often push her to override her own pace, leading her into situations that felt rushed or overwhelming.

Together, we created a new strategy that honored her natural strengths. Nancy stopped chasing connection and began creating it on her own terms. She chose environments and conversations that reflected her values and emotional rhythm. And the shift was powerful. Once she started honoring her own pace and needs, she began attracting men who genuinely appreciated her depth, vulnerability, and presence.

The Freedom of Authenticity

Authenticity gets talked about a lot in dating, but what's often missing is the *how*. Just being yourself isn't always enough if you're repeating old patterns or ignoring your deeper needs. That's where your Love Style becomes a powerful tool. When you pair self-awareness with strategy, you don't just date—you date intentionally.

And here's the beauty of it: When your dating approach is rooted in who you truly are, you naturally attract the kind of connection that fits.

Ask yourself:

- How can I integrate authenticity into my dating strategy?

- What steps can I take to date with intention and alignment?

Key Takeaways:

- Empowered dating starts with aligning your approach to your natural strengths, values, and goals.

- Discovering your Love Style helps you craft a strategy that feels authentic and sustainable.

- Showing up with clarity and authenticity attracts the connections that matter most.

Reflection Exercise:

- **Which Love Style resonated most with you?** Were you surprised, or did your quiz result feel like an "aha" moment?

- **How can you use The Alignment List to support your unique Love Style?** What are some ways you can honor your needs in future conversations or connections?

- Where in your dating life can you add more strategy without losing your authenticity?

Now it's time to shift from seeking to sustaining.

In Phase 5: Nurturing, we'll shift the focus to caring for your whole self—emotionally, mentally, and physically—while dating. Because building a meaningful connection with someone else starts with how you care for yourself.

PHASE 5:
NURTURING

"I will not abandon myself—not for love, not for anything."

— Nedra Glover Tawwab

CHAPTER 12:
FILLING YOUR JOY CUP FIRST

Why Self-Care Is Non-Negotiable

Dating and relationships are deeply emotional experiences, and to show up fully for the journey of love, you need to take care of yourself first. Self-care isn't selfish, it's essential. It's the foundation of healthy love, preparing you for a relationship that thrives while reminding you that you are worthy of love and care, starting with yourself.

When you prioritize your emotional and physical well-being, you're not just preparing for a healthy relationship—you're modeling the kind of love and respect you hope to receive from a partner.

Behind the Shift: Sheila Took a Closer Look at the Love She Had

Sheila came to me while she was still in a relationship. She wasn't actively dating but she was questioning whether she should be. Something felt off, but she couldn't quite articulate what or why.

After taking the Dating Reset quiz, Sheila discovered that her Love Style was the Romantic Optimist. As a hopeful believer in love, she often led with openness and emotional generosity. She wanted to believe the best about men and often did. But her tendency to emotionally invest early meant she sometimes stayed in situations longer than she should, fueled by hope that things would get better.

In her current relationship, she found herself constantly making excuses for behavior that didn't align with what she truly wanted. She believed in his potential, believed in the idea of the relationship, but she didn't always feel emotionally met.

Understanding her Love Style helped Sheila name the pattern. She realized that her optimism, while beautiful, sometimes overpowered her discernment. Instead of focusing on how she felt, she had been focused on what could be.

With this clarity, Sheila began asking deeper questions, not just of him, but of herself. Were their values truly aligned? Was the relationship supporting her emotionally, or was she holding onto potential?

This insight gave her something she didn't even realize she needed: permission to take a step back from nurturing the relationship and start nurturing herself. She no longer felt like she had to hold it all together.

Instead, she turned inward, gave herself space, and reconnected with what she needed to feel safe, seen, and supported.

Filling Your Emotional Cup

Self-care isn't just about bubble baths or spa days (though those are wonderful, too). It's about identifying what nourishes you emotionally, mentally, and physically—and making those practices a priority.

Here are some ways to fill your emotional cup:

1. Set Healthy Boundaries to Protect Your Peace

Protecting your emotional energy is a form of self-love. Boundaries aren't walls—they're filters. They help you discern what's for you and what's not. For Sheila, setting boundaries didn't mean leaving the relationship—it meant learning how to express what she needed in a way she never had before. Through understanding her Love Style and attachment triggers, she began to recognize where she was abandoning her own needs in favor of keeping the peace. Now, she had the language to advocate for herself and the tools to communicate her emotional needs clearly—something she hadn't been aware of or practiced before.

Try this: Ask yourself, "Where am I saying yes when I really mean no?" or "What needs am I quieting in order to avoid conflict?" Then, practice expressing one of those needs with honesty and compassion.

2. Create Daily Rituals That Restore You

Rituals create rhythm. They help you come home to yourself, especially in a world (and dating culture) that can feel chaotic or inconsistent. These don't need to be elaborate. A five-minute morning meditation, an evening cup of tea with no screens, or gratitude journaling before bed can ground you. When you build small moments of restoration into your day, you send yourself the message: I matter.

Try this: Choose one simple ritual to do daily for a week and see how it shifts your energy. It could be lighting a candle before journaling, walking or sitting outside without your phone, or writing one thing you're proud of each night.

3. Be Mindful of Your Inner Dialogue

The way you speak to yourself matters especially when dating can stir up old insecurities or fear-based stories. Being nurturing toward yourself means paying attention to your internal tone. Are you being supportive or self-critical? Are you giving yourself grace, or constantly second-guessing every interaction? Your inner voice sets the tone for how you show up and what you accept.

Try this: Notice what you say to yourself after a date or conversation. Would you speak that way to someone you love? If not, pause, reframe, and replace the thought with something more compassionate: "We're all a work in progress." "I'm proud of how I showed up." "I get to take my time."

Self-Care Through the Lens of Your Love Style

When you understand your Love Style, you don't just learn how you show up in relationships, you also learn how to care for yourself in ways that feel truly restorative. Each Love Style comes with its own emotional strengths and challenges. That's why self-care isn't one-size-fits-all. What nourishes one woman might completely miss the mark for another.

Here's how to fill your emotional cup based on your Love Style:

The Over-Giver

You lead with generosity and tend to give emotionally—sometimes more than you receive.

Your self-care reset: Focus on receiving. Ask yourself, "Where do I need to pull back so I can pour into myself?" Set time aside each week for something that's just for you, no one else.

Supportive practices: Saying no without over-explaining, practicing receiving compliments, and taking solo time without guilt. Even something as simple as letting someone else plan the date or pick up the tab can feel like a radical act of balance.

The Romantic Optimist

You believe in love and want to see the best in people, sometimes investing too quickly.

Your self-care reset: Slow down. Check in with how someone makes you feel, not just what they say. Give yourself space to reflect between interactions instead of jumping to emotionally "fill in the blanks."

Supportive practices: Journaling after dates, voice-noting your thoughts before reaching out, setting a 24-hour pause before making big emotional decisions. Self-care for you is about creating space before you say yes so you can tune into your own pace and not be pulled off your center by theirs.

The Cautious Skeptic

You're practical and protective of your heart, which can sometimes mean staying in your head.

Your self-care reset: Let yourself feel. Trust that opening up doesn't have to mean losing control. It's okay to admit when you're unsure or vulnerable.

Supportive practices: Body-based movement (like yoga or dance), breathwork, or even narrating your feelings to yourself in the mirror.

Self-care for you might be simply noticing when you're shutting down and gently staying present instead.

The Independent Protector

You've worked hard to build your peace and don't give up emotional space easily.

Your self-care reset: Create room for intimacy without it feeling like a threat to your freedom. That starts by nurturing your emotional needs instead of keeping everything self-contained.

Supportive practices: Let someone help you (yes, even with something small), experiment with shared rituals, or try voicing your needs before you've solved them all internally. Self-care here is about letting love in without losing yourself in the process.

Key Takeaways:

- Self-care isn't a luxury; it's a foundational part of choosing and sustaining aligned love.

- Your Love Style offers insight into how you show up emotionally, and how you can best support yourself throughout the dating journey.

- Tending to your emotional needs through rituals, boundaries, and supportive practices helps you stay connected to yourself while staying open to connection with others.

Reflection Exercise:

- Which Love Style do you most resonate with, and how does it influence the way you care for yourself in relationships?

- What emotional or energetic patterns have you noticed that drain you, and how can you start to shift them?

- Choose one self-nurturing ritual or boundary from this chapter that aligns with your Love Style. How will you incorporate it this week?

The next chapter is dedicated to resilience in rejection. Because no matter how confident or clear you are, rejection is part of the dating journey.

CHAPTER 12:

CHAPTER 13:
RESILIENCE IN REJECTION

Rejection and Love Styles

Rejection is a natural part of the dating process, but it can feel deeply personal—especially when it activates attachment-related fears. Recognizing how rejection affects you based on your attachment style can help you navigate these moments with resilience and self-compassion.

Instead of letting rejection define you, what if you let it *refine* you? Each experience has something to teach you about your needs, your desires, and your growth. When viewed with compassion and curiosity, rejection becomes an opportunity to deepen your self-trust, rather than erode it.

Rejection Through the Lens of Your Love Style

Each Love Style responds to rejection in different ways. Understanding your natural tendencies can help you *shift from reaction to reflection* and give you the tools to care for yourself in a way that supports healing, not spiraling.

1. **The Over-Giver** Rejection can feel like confirmation that you weren't "enough" or didn't do enough. You might overanalyze what you gave or where you went wrong.

   What helps: Instead of replaying the relationship, redirect that care inward. Practice affirmations like: *"I don't have to earn love through overgiving."* Reconnect with what you need—not just what you gave.

2. **The Romantic Optimist** You might feel blindsided, especially if you emotionally invested early. Rejection can feel like the loss of not just a person, but the possibility.

   What helps: Give yourself space to feel the disappointment without rushing to reframe it too quickly. Journal your emotions and revisit The Alignment List to remind yourself what's still possible—and why you're worth the wait.

3. **The Cautious Skeptic** Your response may be to shut down or intellectualize the experience to avoid emotional discomfort. You might tell yourself, *"This is why I don't open up."*

   What helps: Let yourself feel it. Even just admitting, "That hurt," is a powerful act of emotional honesty. Connect with someone safe and trusted, or write a reflection to process what this experience taught you.

4. **The Independent Protector** You may withdraw and feel tempted to reinforce emotional walls, using the rejection as a reason to stay self-contained.

What helps: Remind yourself that this doesn't mean vulnerability is unsafe—it means this particular connection wasn't aligned. Return to the practices that center you and gently explore what it would look like to stay open *just enough*.

Building Resilience in the Face of Rejection

Resilience isn't about avoiding rejection, it's about how you respond to it. The next time you face rejection, ask yourself this: *How might this experience be redirecting me toward something better aligned with my values and desires?*

Here are some strategies to help you navigate rejection with strength and grace:

1. **Reframe Rejection**:
   Instead of seeing rejection as a failure, view it as redirection. *It's not about what you've lost but about the clarity you've gained.*

Every 'no' brings you closer to the 'yes' that aligns with your vision for love.

2. **Practice Gratitude:**

   Reflect on what the experience taught you, whether it's a deeper understanding of your needs or a clearer sense of what doesn't work for you. Gratitude helps shift your perspective from loss to growth.

3. **Lean on Your Support System:**

   Talking to a trusted friend or family member, dating or life coach, or therapist can provide perspective, energy, and encouragement. Sharing your feelings aloud can lighten the emotional load and remind you that you're not alone. A trusted advisor who has your greatest good in mind can also help you hear your own inner voice, recognize your lessons learned, and celebrate your journey along the way.

The Power of Self-Compassion

Rejection doesn't define your worth—it's simply a natural part of the journey to finding aligned love. Practicing self-compassion can make all the difference in how you process these moments.

Consider this: If a close friend or family member experienced the same rejection, how would you support and encourage them? How can you offer that same kindness to yourself?

Here are some ways to cultivate self-compassion:

- **Acknowledge Your Feelings**: It's okay to feel hurt or disappointed. Give yourself permission to sit with those emotions without judgment. You can honor your emotions and simultaneously trust that emotions are energy in motion, and this too shall pass.

- **Speak Kindly to Yourself**: Replace critical self-talk with supportive affirmations. For example: "This experience/breakup/rejection/divorce doesn't define me. I'm worthy of love, just as I am."

- **Celebrate Your Courage**: Putting yourself out there takes bravery. Remind yourself that every step forward, even the challenging ones, brings you closer to your goals.

By treating yourself with the kindness and understanding you would offer a loved one, you build resilience and reinforce your sense of self-worth.

Key Takeaways:

- Rejection is a natural part of the dating process, but it doesn't define your worth.

- Each Love Style responds to rejection differently; knowing yours can help you navigate it with clarity and care.

- Resilience starts with reframing rejection as redirection, not failure.

- Returning to The Alignment List reminds you of your values and protects your vision for love.

- Practicing self-compassion is essential to moving forward with confidence and emotional strength.

Reflection Exercise:

- How has rejection impacted your beliefs about love and connection?

- What tools or practices from this chapter can help you reframe rejection in a healthy way?

- Create a Rejection Recovery Plan. Think of it as your emotional first-aid kit. What will help you come back to yourself when rejection stings? Consider things like revisiting your Alignment List, reaching out to a friend, journaling your feelings, dancing it out, or even taking a nap to help you feel centered and cared for.

- Journal about a past rejection. What did you learn from the experience, and how can you use that insight to approach love with greater resilience?

In Phase 6: Gratitude, you'll reflect on your growth with compassion and abundance.

CHAPTER 13:

PHASE 6:
GRATITUDE

"Every time I thought I was being rejected from something good, I was actually being redirected to something better."

— Dr. Caroline Myss

CHAPTER 14:
GRATITUDE AS A FOUNDATION

Gratitude has a remarkable way of transforming how we see the dating journey and ourselves. It's not just about being thankful when things go well. It's about recognizing growth in the messy moments too: the awkward dates, the rejections, and even the heartbreaks.

In the context of dating, gratitude helps us move from a mindset of scarcity—"Why haven't I found love yet?"—to one of abundance: "Look at how far I've come, and what I've learned."

This shift changes everything. You stop measuring your journey by how close you are to the finish line and start valuing how you're showing up along the way.

From Scarcity to Abundance

For years, I believed there were no good men left. I had collected evidence in the form of disappointing relationships, red flags I ignored, and moments of heartbreak that convinced me maybe I was asking for too much. I told myself, "All the good ones are taken," and "Anyone still single over 40 is single for a reason."

That scarcity mindset made dating feel like a losing game. I became hesitant to try, quick to give up, or tempted to settle for less than I knew I deserved.

Everything shifted when I decided to date with gratitude. Instead of focusing on what hadn't happened yet, I began to appreciate the possibilities ahead of me. I reminded myself that rejection was redirection. That a date that didn't lead to love was still a chance to learn something about myself. That the kind of partnership I wanted was real and I was becoming the woman who could receive it.

When I leaned into this mindset, things changed. I opened myself up to new possibilities. I met many great men. And eventually, I chose a partner who was aligned with my values, respected my boundaries, and brought out the best in me.

Client Story: Nancy's Gratitude Practice

In her 50s, Nancy committed to start a gratitude journal just for her dating life. After each date, she jotted down one thing she was grateful for: the courage it took to show up, a kind gesture, a moment of clarity. Even the dates that didn't go anywhere had value; they gave her more insight about herself and what she truly wanted. That simple shift changed her energy and helped her approach dating with much more ease and optimism.

As Nancy put it, "Dating in my 50s is a whole new world. Honestly, I'd never really dated before. I married my high school sweetheart - he liked me, and that was that. Now, I'm grateful to be learning how to date with intention and embracing the idea that I get to choose. I'm much clearer about the man I want in my life."

Reframing Rejection

Gratitude isn't about ignoring your feelings. It's about noticing what's working, even when things don't go the way you hoped.

Gratitude says:

- "Each 'no' brings me closer to the right 'yes.'"

- "Love IS possible and I'm aligning with it every day."

- "Even if something didn't last, it taught me something valuable."

This mindset doesn't minimize the hard parts; it helps you move through them with more grace and less self-blame.

Gratitude Beyond Love

Gratitude isn't limited to dating, it's a lens through which you can view your entire life. When you focus on what you're grateful for, you invite more joy, abundance, and fulfillment into every area.

Here's how to cultivate gratitude beyond your love life:

- **Celebrate Your Wins:** Whether it's setting a boundary, prioritizing self-care, or simply showing up for yourself, honor the small victories that reflect your growth.

- **Nurture Your Passions:** Engage in activities that bring you joy, curiosity, and connection. And when you do those things that light you up, give thanks—before, during, and after.

- **Appreciate the Present:** Spend time with the people and experiences that remind you of the love and abundance already in your life.

Gratitude as Your Foundation

When gratitude becomes your foundation, it shifts your entire journey. It helps you stay present, appreciate the process, and trust that aligned love will arrive at the right time.

Gratitude isn't just about what you've achieved or what's ahead; it's about recognizing the beauty and value of where you are right now.

Key Takeaways:

- Gratitude shifts your focus from scarcity and frustration to growth, clarity, and possibility.

- Reframing rejection as redirection helps you stay open and aligned on your dating journey.

- Practicing gratitude through journaling, reflection, and presence strengthens your emotional resilience and trust in the process.

- Gratitude isn't about ignoring challenges—it's about choosing to see the value in every step.

Reflection Exercise:

- What moments in your dating journey are you most grateful for even if they didn't lead to love?

- Where in your life are you already experiencing abundance, connection, or growth?

- What's one gratitude ritual or practice you'd like to carry forward into your dating life (or beyond)?

Gratitude shifts how you see the journey, but now it's time to celebrate how far you've come. You've done the inner work, stayed curious, and kept showing up, even when it wasn't easy.

In the next chapter, we're going to pause and honor that. Because this version of you? She's not the same woman who started this journey. And she deserves to be seen, felt, and celebrated.

CHAPTER 14:

CHAPTER 15:
HONORING YOUR TRANSFORMATION

As you've moved through this book, you've untangled patterns, clarified what you want, and deepened your connection to yourself. Now it's time to pause and truly honor the woman you've become.

Transformation doesn't always show up as loud victories. Sometimes, it's in the quiet moments where you chose yourself. The boundary you finally held. The date you walked away from because it didn't feel aligned. The courage to keep your heart open.

This chapter is about celebrating the small, powerful shifts that mark your growth and looking at your progress through the lens of gratitude.

Signs You've Grown

- **New Patterns**: You're no longer chasing misaligned partners or ignoring red flags.

- **Clarity**: You know what you value and what you won't

compromise on.

- **Resilience**: You bounce back more quickly. You trust yourself more.

- **Authenticity**: You're dating as your full self, not shrinking or shape-shifting to be chosen.

Reflection: Who You Were vs. Who You Are Now

Think back to the version of you who started this journey. Maybe she was tired, unsure, or afraid to try again. Now think about who you are today. You've made decisions rooted in alignment. You've shown up with intention. You've become more grounded, more open, more you.

You didn't just learn how to date.

You learned how to trust yourself.

Client Story: Keisha's Milestone Moment

Keisha celebrated the end of her Dating Reset by curling up in her favorite cozy corner and rereading the journal entries she had written from the very beginning. She was so glad she had stuck with it because writing her insights down gave her a clear window into her growth. As she turned the pages, she could see just how much her thinking had shifted. She noticed how differently she now responds to situations that once left her feeling unsure or off balance.

For Keisha, the milestone wasn't about a grand gesture. It was about recognizing the internal transformation she had created, one page at a time.

Key Takeaways:

- You've evolved, emotionally, mentally, and spiritually, and that transformation deserves celebration.

- Growth shows up in small but powerful ways, like new boundaries, clearer choices, deeper self-care, and more confidence in who you are.

- Reflecting on who you were and who you are now helps reinforce your self-trust and alignment.

- You don't need external validation to mark your progress. Your inner shifts are worth honoring.

Reflection Exercise:

- What's one choice you made during this journey that you're really proud of?

- How has your relationship with yourself changed since starting this book?

- Write a short note to your past self, acknowledging her courage and letting her know how far she's come.

- Create a Personal Milestone: Whether it's treating yourself to something meaningful (a self-love ring or necklace, a special dress, etc.), lighting a candle, getting a massage, or going to a wellness retreat, choose a way to honor your progress with intention.

You are not the same woman who started this journey. You've grown, you've softened, you've strengthened and now…you're ready.

CHAPTER 15:

CONCLUSION: YOUR PATH TO LOVE

The Journey to Aligned Love

As you reach the end of this book, take a deep breath and reflect on the path you've walked. Each lesson, each moment of self-discovery, and every intentional choice you've made has brought you closer to the love you desire.

This journey was never just about dating. It was about understanding who you truly are, transforming how you see yourself, your worth, and your relationships.

It was about aligning with your values, embracing your authenticity, and creating space for a partnership that reflects what you want and need.

You Are Already Enough

One truth I hope you carry with you is this: You are already enough.

You don't need to fix, change, or shrink yourself to find love.

The love you desire doesn't demand perfection; it invites you to be present, intentional, and true to yourself.

Throughout this journey, you've gained the tools and clarity to not just attract love but to build it upon a foundation of alignment, gratitude, and authenticity.

Embracing Abundance

As you move forward, I encourage you to approach love with a mindset of abundance. The world is full of men who are looking for the same kind of love you are—partnerships built on mutual respect, joy, growth, and genuine connection.

The stories I've shared show what's possible when you trust your values and your journey. With each experience, you gain clarity, resilience, and a deeper understanding of what truly aligns with you.

When you embrace abundance, you release your grip on fear, scarcity, and pressure. You trust that everything you need is already within you—and that when the right connection comes, you'll recognize it instead of dismissing or fearing it.

Not Luck, A Mindset Shift

You may remember the story I shared about how I met my husband and how that connection only happened because I chose to date differently.

That shift wasn't about luck. It was about clarity, self-trust, and showing up with curiosity, getting to know him without rushing to commit.

And with that mindset, I could remember something essential: We're all carrying something. A story. A fear. A hope.

You can hold space for that in someone else without abandoning your own needs. Compassion and boundaries can co-exist.

Because the truth is—we're all looking for our person. And we're all worthy of a love that's rooted, expansive, and deeply mutual.

The Path Forward

Your journey doesn't end here. It begins anew, with a deeper understanding of yourself and a clearer vision for the love you desire.

Aligned love isn't a destination. It's a way of living, loving, and being. As you walk this path forward, trust in your growth, your alignment, and the abundance waiting for you. You deserve every beautiful connection this journey brings.

Your Story, Your Power

The love you desire begins with you. Your courage, your clarity, and your commitment to alignment are your greatest strengths.

As you continue, remember: *You are the love you have been searching for, and the right partner will only add to the joy you have built within yourself.*

This is your aligned path forward. Step into it with confidence, gratitude, and the knowledge that you are ready for the love you've always desired.

> *"You're not too old, you're not broken, and you're definitely not alone. The love you desire is possible, and it begins with understanding yourself, staying open to truly getting to know him, and honoring your boundaries along the way. Dating at this stage of life is layered, it's nuanced, and it requires a different kind of clarity, but you're more than capable of navigating it with intention and grace."*
>
> —Nadia Edwards

THANK YOUS

To my late mother, Sonia K. Symister:

Thank you for showing me love in the best way you knew how and for teaching me the resilience to navigate this world. You are still my hero. Your love and strength continue to guide me. *Walk good.*

To my extraordinary husband, Jake:

Thank you for being my safe place, my sounding board, and the love I waited for. Your steady presence and belief in me have carried me through the quiet moments and the big leaps. You remind me every day what true life partnership is.

To my incredible son, Takaris:

Thank you for your quiet strength, your thoughtfulness, and your presence. Watching you move through the world with integrity and heart makes me proud every single day. Your encouragement throughout this journey meant more to me than you know.

To my friends and family:

Your encouragement carried me through the highs and lows of this process. Thank you for always being in my corner and for lovingly reminding me of my own lessons when I needed them most.

To my clients and community:

Your stories, your struggles, and your breakthroughs have been my greatest inspiration. Thank you for trusting me with your journey. It is an honor to walk alongside you.

And finally, to you, the reader:

The fact that you picked up this book means you're ready for something new. I'm so honored to be a part of your path. May you find love that feels intentional, expansive, and truly yours.

WORK WITH NADIA

DO YOU WANT TO...

- Stop second-guessing yourself and start dating with clarity and confidence?

- Rebuild trust in your own decisions and desires?

- Experience dating as a space of emotional safety — not stress or exhaustion?

- Attract love that aligns with the woman you are now, not who you used to be?

Whatever your story, you're not too late and you're not alone.

You just need the right support and better guidance than what you've been given before.

If you connected with *The Dating Reset* and want to go deeper, here are three powerful ways we can work together:

1. THE REDEFINING LOVE JOURNEY

A transformational coaching experience for women 40+ ready to detach from old patterns, rebuild self-trust, and date with joy and confidence.

Inside this guided group container, you'll learn how to release fear, shift your mindset, and show up fully aligned in a powerful community of women doing the same.

Join the waitlist at www.NadiaEdwards.com/waitlist or scan the QR code.

2. SECRETS TO CHOOSING ALIGNED LOVE

A bite-sized, self paced on-demand video series — perfect if you want a quick, powerful mindset shift.

In under an hour, you'll learn key strategies, journaling prompts, and practical steps to help you reset your dating approach and start choosing aligned love.

Learn more or get started at www.NadiaEdwards.com/reset or get started now by scanning the QR code.

3. BOOK A CALL TO EXPLORE OPTIONS

Not sure which path is right for you? Let's talk it through.

If you're curious about working with me but prefer a more personalized or high-touch experience I invite you to book a call.

We'll meet one-on-one to discuss where you are in your dating journey and what kind of support would serve you best. Whether it's group coaching or a private intensive, this conversation will help.

Schedule your call at: www.NadiaEdwards.com/call

Let's find what's aligned and build something beautiful from here.

ABOUT THE AUTHOR

Nadia Edwards is a sought-after dating clarity and relationship expert, speaker, and content creator who specializes in helping single women over 40 find lasting love. With a compassionate yet no-nonsense approach, she empowers women to break unhealthy dating patterns, build confidence and self-love, and make more intentional choices in their love lives.

Drawing from her own experience of finding her life partner in just 30 days, Nadia brings both personal insight and proven strategies to her work. Through her YouTube channel, *Redefining Love After 40 with Nadia Edwards,* and the *Grown and Tender* podcast, she explores topics like modern dating, financial compatibility, attachment styles, boundaries, communication, and relationship dynamics, helping women navigate love with clarity and purpose.

When she's not sharing dating insights, she enjoys traveling the world with her husband while inspiring others to find the deep, fulfilling love they deserve.

Connect with Nadia and learn more at: **www.NadiaEdwards.com**

Discover your Love Style and take the Dating Reset Quiz at:

www.NadiaEdwards.com/quiz

Grown and Tender podcast is on Spotify and Apple

YouTube: ***Redefining Love After 40 with Nadia Edwards***

Instagram: **@iamnadiaedwards**

If *The Dating Reset* resonated with you, I'd be grateful if you left a five-star review on Amazon or wherever you purchased the book. Reviews help more women over 40 discover that aligned love isn't behind them—it's still ahead. And if you have a friend who needs that reminder? Share this book with her. We're in this together.

Nadia ♥

www.ingramcontent.com/pod-product-compliance
Lightning Source LLC
Chambersburg PA
CBHW020543030426
42337CB00013B/953